Wonderstruck
by Art & Artists

Other Books by Greg Wright

Tolkien in Perspective
Peter Jackson in Perspective
Two Roads Through Narnia
A Narnia Glossary of Obscure Terms
The Da Vinci Code Adventure
West of the Gospel
The Gospel of Doubt
What I Want for You

Wonderstruck
Wonderstruck by The Methow

Wonderstruck
by Art & Artists

because the universe wants us to be in awe of what comes next

Greg Wright

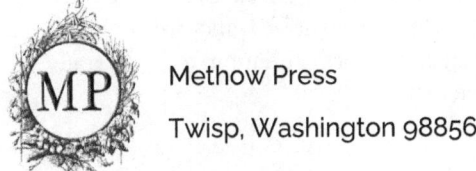

Methow Press
Twisp, Washington 98856

© 2018-2025 by Greg Wright

Published by Methow Press
P.O. Box 1213, Twisp, WA 98856
www.methowpress.com

Printed in the United States of America

All rights reserved. No part of this publication may be reproduced, stored in a retrieval system, or transmitted in any form or by any means—for example, electronic, photocopy, or recording—without the prior written permission of the publisher. The only exception is brief quotations in printed reviews.

Essays in this work have appeared previously on Facebook and Medium.

ISBN: 979-8-9913567-5-6

Cover image courtesy NASA.

Unless otherwise noted, all Scripture quotations in this work are from The Holy Bible, New International Version ® NIV ® Copyright © 1973, 1978, 1984 by the International Bible Society. All rights reserved.

Extended quotes from books, songs, and poetry written by the author's friends and associates have been used by permission. Other quotes from works by public figures are used under Fair Use provisions of U.S. copyright law and are intended, as a form of scholarly critique, to draw attention to and praise the works of those public figures.

Contents

Introduction i	Nathan Clark George 73
Soundtrack Shuffle 1	Hill and Stone 76
Avelange 3	Henry Poole 79
Millennials 5	Skybound Blue 87
Widmung 9	The New World 89
MaMuse 11	Church of the Beloved 94
Freddy & Francine 13	Glenn Miller 97
The Moody Blues 15	Sway Wild 101
Emi Meyer 17	Free Solo 104
Ennio Morricone 19	Francis Thompson 107
Paul Simon 22	The Lord of the Rings 114
Jason Gray 24	Winterlings 119
Holly Hunter 27	Billy Knapp 122
Ginny Owens 31	Ajeet Kaur 125
Elvis Costello 34	Keith Parkes 128
The Untouchables 38	Mindwalk 131
Cris Krusen 44	Styx 135
Jake Gyllenhaal 46	Emmanuel 138
Warren Etheredge 49	Bill Murray 142
Keri Russell 52	Springsteen 146
Jim Carrey 55	Temptation 149
Boadicea 59	1812 154
Brian May 61	Dissonance 156
Queen 64	The Fault in Our Stars 160
Kevin Costner 68	Hollywood Jesus 162
Bill Paxton 70	George Harrison 167

C.S. Lewis 170	Michael Mann 227
Roger Taylor 175	Zhivago 231
Lee and Bianca 178	Nuremburg 234
Southside 182	Jesus 238
E.B. White 186	Robert Guiry 242
The Council of Elrond 191	Equinox 244
Ben-Hur 194	Tolkien 246
Friedkin 197	The Railway Man 249
Michael Kamen 201	The Imitation Game 253
Jesus of Montreal 203	Simple Men 258
Tupelo Bar 206	Herb Alpert 261
Thresholds 209	Miss American Pie 267
Albert Lewin 211	Whiplash 271
Apophenia 214	Never Cry Wolf 275
Merry Gentlemen 218	Acknowledgements 279
Elf 222	

Introduction

After my wife, Jenn, passed away at the end of 2017 in the wake of nearly fifteen years of terminal illness, I began writing a series of letters to her on a Facebook page titled "Memos to the Missus." The tagline was "Because who else would I tell?"

From that grew the first Wonderstruck essay, an exceedingly brief reflection on my April 2018 raft trip through the Grand Canyon and a performance of Ferde Grofé's "Grand Canyon Suite" by the Auburn, Washington, Symphony—an unexpected treat as part of a musical program co-hosted by performance artist and friend Adrian Wyard.

The essays which followed are unapologetically optimistic and have been predicated on a profound belief that life is not entirely random… and that the intention of the universal and infinite works itself out through the interactions that we have with one another and all the world around us.

Christopher Hitchens believed that the credulous are so because they have rehearsed their minds to accept as miraculous what is patently impossible. He is probably correct; but those who rehearse their minds to reject the possibility of the miraculous are missing many wondrous things because they have rehearsed their minds to do so.

Long before I discovered the film *Wonderstruck* on a day filled with serendipity and synchronicity, my mind and soul had been rehearsed for acceptance of the wondrous because of the consumption of art. I grew up on a steady diet of high-quality films, literature, and music. And as you probably know, if you have lifted this tome to read, art of all kinds is filled with turns of joy, rapture, and chills.

Yes, you come to expect it. And when it comes, because you have expected it, because you have been paying attention and waiting… well, you can be wonderstruck.

I was further inculcated by formal study of the arts: poetry, literature, and film. I later taught literature, film, and theater at the college level, and also worked as a movie and pop-culture reviewer for twenty years.

So, yes: I was already predisposed to find wondrous things in art and artists themselves. As my writing became more creative and less clinical, I also came to grips with the idea that I, too, am an artist—not merely an appreciative member of the audience.

Still, my encounter with the film *Wonderstruck* and the circumstances surrounding that encounter—documented in my book *Wonderstruck*—had a profound effect on how I have come to interact with artists and their work. My approach is now much more personal, and the joy, rapture, and chills from the dramatic turns have become more intense. The essays in this collection demonstrate that intensity—documents of divine appointments and magic moments rather than reviews or critiques *per se*.

And yet I hope that the words I say about these works and their makers lead you to seek some of them out for yourself.

Everything that you read in these pages is 100% true, if much of it wildly improbable. I have lived my questions, as Rilke once recommended to a young poet, and these essays are a record of my progress, gradually, without perhaps even noticing it, toward living into my own answers.

I invite you to question my experience, to ponder whether such a universe can actually exist.

But be patient with my words, especially if they resonate, and read them slowly. And also be patient with your own journey as you live your own questions.

Greg Wright
Winthrop, Washington
December 1, 2024

Soundtrack Shuffle

I've been driving a lot more than usual the last few months, and that means I've been listening to music a lot, too. And really *listening*. I can focus more on music when I'm behind the wheel than when I'm at home.

The last few days I've had my MP3 player on the "shuffle" setting... with my Film Score genre selected. When the idea first occurred to me, I thought it was ridiculous... hopping randomly from Ennio Morricone to Howard Shore to Danny Elfman to Bruce Broughton to Maurice Jarre and so on. How jarring that would be!

But my appetite for the unexpected got the better of me, so I went ahead and pressed the Shuffle button. What an awesome surprise!

Music, like the other arts, is predicated on deliberate surprise—of working with expected, familiar keys, chords, and note progressions, all within familiar forms. And then twisting all those conventions in very specific ways to make the experience memorable—and powerful. It's a glorious dance of predictability and wonder.

It's not surprising, then, to find that I tend to listen to music in the same way: wanting surprises, but wanting them to be more controlled than random. Classic Rock shuffle doesn't bother us, of course, because that's how we're used to being fed that stuff on the radio. Maybe even Classical shuffle, if one is used to listening to Classical radio. (As long as we don't shuffle symphony or concerto movements!)

But soundtracks?

How many of us even listen to soundtracks? And if we do, how many just grab a track or two? Naw, we like to listen to them, when we do, from beginning to end, in just the same sequence we heard the music when we saw the film. It can almost be like playing the film back in fast-forward. Or skipping commercials on TiVo or something.

So, yeah... Soundtrack Shuffle is a bit of an odd concept.

What I've found, though, is that the experience is not unlike driving itself—always kind of knowing where you're going, but always an element of the unexpected to go along with it.

Will you miss the light? Will you encounter a traffic slowdown? Will that truck ahead of you to the right throw a chunk of tire cap right into your windshield? Will you round a corner and be blinded by the sun? Or a stunning view? Or a deer bounding across the road, or grazing in a meadow?

So Film Score Shuffle complements the driving experience in a delightful way. Kind of a surprise layer cake. Yummy!

Today's most startling (and pleasing) sequence:
- Charles-Henri Avelange's "Awakening," *Age of Heroes*
- Klaus Badelt's "Walk the Plank," *Pirates of the Caribbean*
- Morricone's "Burning Village," *Guns for San Sebastian*
- Danny Elfman's "Edward Meets the World," *Edward Scissorhands*

Avelange

Well, my composer friend and former colleague Charles-Henri Avelange was certainly floored by yesterday's Wonderstruck note about Soundtrack Shuffle.

I mentioned at the close of that note about his track "The Awakening" leading off a remarkable sequence of tunes. He noted the following not long after I posted:

> Sometimes life can be quite amazing and odd...
>
> I actually have a hard time to express what's going on right now: Today, after not touching *Age Of Heroes* for a decade, I decided to revisit it for a potential concert. The first theme I decided to work on? THE AWAKENING. [Capitals his.]
>
> And then as I take a break I notice on my phone that someone tagged me on Facebook. And I read your post, Greg. And the chills just won't stop. The coincidence is almost scary.
>
> And as proof, I am posting here for you a video of the very "Awakening" that I am working on as we speak.
>
> I am so glad you enjoy listening to my music, and it seems that a higher power is at work here.

I'd certainly like to take credit in some fashion for being at least the conduit of divine affirmation, or something, but the fact is... well, this whole Wonderstruck concept which has been working its way into my brain for the last two months has been the product of a long sequence of hyperventilation-inducing "almost scary" coincidences.

I didn't do anything magical by rocking Charles-Henri's world yesterday. I just paid that sense of wonder forward a little.

Without having any idea what I was doing.

■

Millennials

This morning, my friend and former colleague at *Hollywood Jesus*, Mark Allen Sommer, reposted his *ScreenFish* coverage of *Millennials*, a TV program aired by Ovation a couple years ago.

In *Millennials*, "award-winning producer Rick Stevenson follows the lives of a diverse group of children as they transition from the innocence of childhood into the turbulence of adolescence and into young adults." Topics covered include cutting, drug abuse, gender identity, peer pressure, popularity, immigration, abandonment, and much more.

I am credited in the program as part of the "Bloom Team," Chief Technologist for the company that has developed the process by which stories such as these are captured. Mark caught the reference when he reviewed advance copies of several episodes, and he emailed me to conduct an interview about the series.

The end of the exchange goes as follows:

> MAS: What are some things of spiritual importance we should be looking for as we watch the show?

> GW: Judge not lest ye be judged. Seriously. Right now, the Church seems to be retreating into isolationist rhetoric because it's scared about the societal impacts of gender-neutral bathrooms, the Internet, hook-up culture, and drugs.

But guess what? The damage has already been done. Long ago.

The pressures of our increasingly artificial and disconnected culture have wrought immeasurable damage on us and on our kids. While we're worrying about digging in or casting stones, the kids right next to us are dying on the vine—and what they need is an ear that listens and a heart that feels. And a lot of patience and prayer.

Children do not mature overnight; and all we can say about anyone's path toward God at any given point in time is very limited. The proverb says, "Train up a child in the way he should go, and when he is old he will not depart from it." In the meantime, however, there's a lot of pain and wandering.

You can't really prevent the "Prodigal Child" from self-destruction—but you can be the Prodigal Parent waiting with welcome and open arms when the wanderer returns home.

You might also consider venturing out to the pigsty from time to time as a show of support. Ivory-tower Christians are not modeling the Jesus I know. He met people where they were and loved them.

MAS: Is there anything else you would like us to know about the show and The School of Life Project in general?

GW: Honestly, as I think about my work with the Bloom Method, I often lay awake at night and wonder, "How would my life be different if I had access to this when I was ten and being bullied, or twelve and first getting hooked on porn?"

And I have to remind myself that you can't really play the "What if?" game. My wife, Jenn, and I both led lives not a great deal unlike those featured in *Millennials*—which, as it turned out, God used as the means for us to be of great help to each other as adults. God redeemed it all, because he's the one who is "able to do immeasurably more than all we can ask or imagine." That's the business he's in.

So the obvious answer to my "What if?" is: I wouldn't have married Jenn, and we wouldn't have shared the rich spiritual heritage that we did.

But God's power is also no excuse for us to turn a blind eye to the suffering that's around us or bury our heads in the sand and pretend it's not there at all. I can say without hesitation that it's better for a girl to stop cutting on herself today than five years from now, or for a boy to start developing healthy connections with real girls at sixteen rather than at thirty-six.

And those are the paths of healing, restoration, and reconciliation that the Bloom Method is trying to open up. Kids need to know that they're not weird and that they're not alone. And they need to know there's a hope and a future. That's what we hope is communicated through *Millennials*.

It so happens that Mark reran this interview the morning that Rick and I and the rest of "the Bloom Team" concluded a three-day series of meetings about how to reorganize the company and take the project to the next level—as StoryQ.

Part of those discussions centered around what to do with *Millennials* and *LISTEN* and other films in our library.

It's powerful to know that people are still paying attention!

■

Widmung

I made it almost entirely through my workday yesterday without turning on a shred of music. Inconceivable!

I admit that my mind was a little distracted, what with it being my late wife Jenn's birthday and with family plans for a memorial butterfly release in the offing. Nonetheless, about 4 PM I suddenly remembered that I should have some music playing.

I picked up my MP3 player and was about to pick an album when the thought came to me, "Wait! I should let this be a surprise!" So I hit the Random button and let the player select for me.

The player picked Robert Schumann's piano arrangement of "Widmung" (*Du meine Seele, du mein Herz*, Of My Heart, Of My Soul).

Uh huh. I've probably listened to that track once before, having just picked up the CD at a thrift store with Jenn last spring. I certainly have never seen the title before.

Here's what I learned about the song by Googling:

> Schumann's "Widmung" (Dedication) opens his song-cycle "Myrthen" (Myrtles), which was appropriately named after the blossoms traditionally associated with marriage festivals, as it was his wedding present to his bride, Clara Wieck.

He began composing songs as a means of proving his financial stability as a future husband, and in "Widmung," as was the case with all his compositions of this genre, he deeply expressed his most heart-felt emotions: passion and devotion, fears and longing, frustration and suffering from their separation, and the hopes and dreams of their life together. He began the cycle in the early part of 1840, finishing it in April, well ahead of his self-established September deadline.

When complete, "Widmung" and its accompanying poems were lavishly bound with a red velvet inscription, which affectionately read "To my beloved bride."

And here's what the lyrics of "Dedication" mean in English:

You my soul, you my heart, you my bliss, O you my pain, you my world in which I live, my heaven you, to which I float, O you my grave, into which my grief forever I've consigned. You are repose, you are peace, you are bestowed on me from Heaven. Your love for me gives me my worth, your eyes transfigure me in mine, lovingly you raise me above myself, my good spirit, my better self!

I guess that's what happens when you ask for surprises!

■

MaMuse

I first encountered Karisha Longaker and Sarah Nutting in Robbers Roost Bookstore in Torrey, Utah, in October of 2008.

Jenn and I were staying at The Lodge at Red River Ranch to celebrate the 10th anniversary of our engagement, and Jenn—in the throes of post-disability depression—had just decided to reinvent herself as a photographer. One of her most-sold photos, "Eden," is a shot of the creek that runs by the bookstore's parking area, a photograph taken that day.

We were inside browsing the shelves with about three other people when a trio of dusty travelers drifted quietly into the store. They conferred briefly with the shop owner and then left. Shortly, Longaker and Nutting returned with a stand-up bass and mandolin and performed an impromptu concert.

The encounter was absolutely astounding, one I've written about in other contexts. It was as if two angels dropped out of heaven… and it was not the first angelic experience we had in Torrey.

Longaker has talked in concerts about how that moment of wonderstruck awe had come about. MaMuse had just cut their first tracks on a home-brew EP CD, and their producer, "a very strange and wonderful man," encouraged them to join him on a cross-country trek to Nashville to record their first album.

"He's the kind of guy who left home very early in life and traveled all over the United States just exploring. So he knows all these caves and hot springs and places to go."

One of these magic places was just outside Torrey, where they had spent the night. Hence their dusty entrance into Robbers Roost.

Over the years, MaMuse has continued to speak into my soul... and at the most opportune and divinely inspired moments. Like last evening, as they sang:

> I have been travelin'
> On a road without answers
> It is not paved
> Nor fenced along the sides
> …
> We are falling
> We are falling
> Into the Arms of Faith

■

Freddy & Francine

Since the evening of January 30, the folk/alt/blues/pop duo Freddy & Francine has been regularly kicking my backside with wonderstruck moment after wonderstruck moment.

And that is soooooo appropriate given that one of those wonderstruck moments had to do with their song "The Moment" off their most recent album *Gung Ho*.

I saw them perform at St. Andrew's House following a spectacular winter hike on the Upper Big Creek loop trail near Lake Cushman. I had just beaten the darkness back to the car after a five-mile epic trek for which I was woefully underprepared, and then driven to Union after a cleanup and quick bite in Hoodsport. As I settled in for F&F's first soulful set, I realized I was experiencing one of the most extraordinary days of my life. They opened with "If You Want Me," which serendipitously also happens to be playing as I am typing this.

I may tell the whole story, someday, about my experience with "The Moment"... but for today, it's enough to tell you about being wonderstruck during last night's online hour-long set that F&F performed live from their Nashville living room couch. They're working on a new album and did this mini-concert to say thanks to their Kickstarter backers.

The subject of the goodness of life has been on my mind a lot lately, and during their set the duo debuted a new song,

"Something Good." I think my notes are right that the closing riff in the chorus is, "I'm tired of being misunderstood / Been fighting all my life just to feel something good."

I'll cop to having my overflowing share of goodness in this life. But as MaMuse sings, "Good is… and goodness is to come." Yes, something good this way comes. Something very good.

Says F&F:

> What we gonna do now
> Our love's on the line
> …
> To make it right
> We've got to hope… to find the time

∎

The Moody Blues

My older brother, Bob, likes to take credit for a lot of the ways that I have developed from a scrawny, whiny, poor-loser runt into a creative, responsible adult.

One thing he can most certainly take credit for, however, is introducing me to The Moody Blues while I was in high school. When I went off to college, one of my first album purchases was my own copy of their double greatest-hits LP *This is The Moody Blues*. I went on to find original releases of all seven of their albums. (By 1979, they had been disbanded for years.)

These days, I'm really happy that the band has finally been enshrined in the Rock 'n' Roll Hall of Fame, since maybe that will convince Justin Hayward, John Lodge, and Graeme Edge to join their fellow original bandmates in retirement. The Moodies have been running on fumes for a looooong time.

Now that I am an old codger myself, I am not as generally enthralled with their brand of psychedelic pop-psychology rock as I once was... but many of their songs still take my breath away. One of those is "Question," particularly the middle "movement" of the song, which breaks from the up-tempo "Why do we never get an answer" opening/closing sections to laze into a plaintive, contemplative groove.

In years past, from when I was as young as sixteen, the principal appeal of the lyric was the "where do I go from here" thrust… and just six months ago, the song crushed me with its prescient insight into tragic loss.

Saturday morning, however, I was overwhelmed by Justin Hayward's confidence in a future of hope restored.

> Between the silence of the mountains
> And the crashing of the sea
> There lies a land I once lived in
> And she's waiting there for me
> …
> I'm looking for someone to change my life
> I'm looking for a miracle in my life
> …
> It's not the way that you say it
> When you do those things to me
> It's more the way you really mean it
> When you tell me what will be

Goodness is, and goodness is to come…

∎

Emi Meyer

Back in 2011 I was sent a review copy of Emi Meyer's album *Suitcase of Stones*.

I was immediately taken with the Japanese-American singer/musician's funky jazz-infused tunes and quirky lyrics. The album always manages to get me into a reflective and gentle mood, and I have followed Meyer's career since.

In 2013, she released *Galaxy's Skirt*, which was just as delightful. The other morning I was enjoying the sun on an open porch with the most excellent of company, and queued up the album. The opening lines of the title track are pretty arresting.

> Strange how we work
> Peeked up the galaxy's skirt
> She told me I was brave

You may have heard of "poetic license." It's the wiggle room that artists get to say things, and say them in ways, that other people aren't allowed to. So, yeah... So yeah, some loaded lyrics there.

But if you allow yourself the liberty to explore the image... in the context of the pregnant purity and grace of unfettered, divinely endowed sexuality and innocence... Well, Meyer goes there.

> Now I fall in love
> Everything I catch a glimpse of
> It reminds me of her

This is the universe that calls to me, and to you: a galaxy of galaxies if you will, a skirt full of Milky Ways… a skirt full of wonder and surprise.

I wonder if Meyer has been in the back of my head for the last five years and has only recently been breaking through into my frontal cortex. "Strange how we work."

> Will you always do those things you do to me
> Oooh, will you always be another mystery
> Please

■

Ennio Morricone

I imagine that the first time I truly fell in love with Morricone's film scores was a screening of *The Good, the Bad and the Ugly* (GB&U) at the Neptune Theater in the University District, or perhaps my first screening of *Once Upon a Time in the West* at the King Theater in downtown Seattle.

Certainly, by the time the opening credits of *The Untouchables* rolled at the Uptown Theater in 1987, I was long hooked. By 1990, I was a full-blown insane Morricone soundtrack collector.

Several thousand dollars later, following epic road trips to collectable vinyl shops in cities such as San Francisco, Detroit, New Orleans, Los Angeles, Manhattan, and Kansas City, I had to give up collecting altogether as I was amassing titles faster than I could listen to them. I was doing pretty well, though, having checked off something like 120 of the 200+ scores Morricone had published on LP.

I had grown up, of course, like just about every other kid my age, with that insane theme from GB&U lodged in my skull... but witnessing the operatic mayhem of Sergio Leone's signature Westerns on the big screen is about the ideal way to grasp the true scope of Morricone's aural vision. And it's not surprising; by the time Leone shot GB&U in 1965, he was already having Morricone pre-score certain sequences in his films, so that the film was cut to the music rather than the other way around.

"The Ecstasy of Gold," which anchors the climax of GB&U, is an absolutely sublime sequence which illustrates the power of the approach.

This morning, my musically literate friend, Chuck Schwanke, posted the most remarkable video on his timeline: the Danish National Symphony performing "The Good, the Bad and the Ugly Suite." I just about died in my office chair as orchestra, chorus, and featured voices brilliantly performed the main title track.

And then I was simply overwhelmed, and wept, as the Suite segued into "The Ecstasy of Gold." Oh, my.

Oh… my. It's playing again as I type these words. Not only is the music just about the most moving score I have ever heard, the Danish National Symphony's staging of their performance is just brilliant. It's wonderful that 21st-century symphonies are finally discovering the power of the twentieth century's orchestral masterworks.

But what is it that strikes me about Morricone's scores, precisely? I think it's his unique combination of classical motifs and things wild. He has said in interviews that he never deliberately wrote scores for obtuse instrumentation; rather, he simply wrote to utilize the best musicians and vocalists available.

Morricone also recognized that the human voice is a brilliant instrument on its own, even when it doesn't utter words.

Just Sunday night as I was driving from Anacortes to Des Moines, I was listening to Howard Shore's *Lord of the Rings* scores and thinking they might have to dislodge GB&U as my favorite driving music.

Huh-uh. The Danish National Symphony has me wonderstruck by "The Ecstasy of Gold" once again.

Thanks, Chuck!

■

Paul Simon

Paul Simon is something like a national treasure.

I don't think that statement needs much defense or warrants a lot of explanation. Anybody whose art and person age as gracefully could be classified as such.

Of course, I know absolutely nothing about the man, personally. He could be another Harvey Weinstein, for all I know. (Then again, Weinstein could be another Simon, for all I know!)

But what I do know is how his art affects me. Kind of like this:

> The cool, cool river
> Sweeps the wild, white ocean
> The rage, the rage of love turns inward
> To become prayers of devotion
> ...
> These prayers are the memory of God
> The memory of God

Not everything Simon has written has the effect or feeling of a prayer, or a memory of God, or the rage of love. But as a body of work? Yes.

And this one song in particular, "Cool, Cool River," from *Rhythm of the Saints*, affects me deeply every time I hear it. It evokes two things within me: the sense-memory of sore loss, closely coupled with a welling desire for something on the other side of loss.

> I believe in the future
> We shall suffer no more
> ...
> And these streets
> Quiet as a sleeping army
> Send their battered dreams to heaven, to heaven
> For the mother's restless son

The album generates its own momentum driving toward "Cool, Cool River," but the song itself has the saintly rhythm of still waters running deep, then swiftly hurtling forward toward the cataract of its musical and thematic conclusion about that "restless son" who says, "Hard times? I'm used to them." The song is a blatant act of defiance in the face of hardness and sorrow, a refusal to accept the voice that says, "This is all we know. And my own immediate sorrow is the center of everyone's universe."

And it works—and Simon's music generally works—because it knows that the song itself, indeed any song on its own, is incomplete without the listener's response. This song, more than most.

> And sometimes even music
> Cannot substitute for tears

No. But music may help release those tears, so that they may mingle in the swirling waters of that cool, cool river...

■

Jason Gray

I am at times very surprised by the things I do not know. Perhaps today's post should be entitled "Dumbstruck" rather than "Wonderstruck"!

> Winter can make us wonder if spring was ever true
> But every winter breaks upon the Easter lily's bloom
> Could it be everything sad is coming untrue?
> Could you believe everything sad is coming untrue?

I own exactly one Jason Gray album. I didn't even buy it. It was yet another CD sent in the mail because some publicist thought that I was in the business of writing music reviews… or hoped that I might start. The title of the album: *Everything Sad Is Coming Untrue*.

My habit with these review-copy CDs was to listen to them once. If nothing grabbed me the first time through, out it went. If something appealed to me on first listen, it would go into the "listen again sometime" stack. If the second time through appealed to me, I'd rip to MP3 and add it to the collection. Could it be everything sad is coming untrue?

> Oh, I believe everything sad is coming untrue
> In the hands of the one who is making all things new

This disc by Jason Gray not only made its way onto my MP3 player, I give it a digital spin every few months. It appeals to me enough that I really probably ought to consider buying one of Gray's albums sometime!

In any event, when I played the album again yesterday, I was not only struck by the lyric to the title track; I was also struck by the ways in which his—or rather, God's—vision for wholeness is playing out in the lives of those close to me.

> The trees look greener, the sky's an ocean
> The world is washed and starting over

And then... I was dumbstruck. In all these years, I had never realized why the album and song title seemed so darned familiar. The words were not written by Jason Gray; they were written by J.R.R. Tolkien.

> "Gandalf! I thought you were dead! But then I thought I was dead myself. Is everything sad going to come untrue? What's happened to the world?"
>
> "A great Shadow has departed," said Gandalf, and then he laughed and the sound was like music, or like water in a parched land; and as he listened the thought came to Sam that he had not heard laughter, the pure sound of merriment, for days upon days without count.

Yes, I should have known better all these years; but perhaps it's fitting that I am reminded now of laughter like the sound of water in a parched land. Sorrow is real and not just some bad dream; but great shadows indeed depart, and they do not define the truth of things. Tolkien had it right in *The Return of the King* (a literary metaphor if there ever was one), and Jason Gray adapted it beautifully and musically:

When the storm leaves there's a silence
That says you don't have to fear anymore

∎

Holly Hunter

> You could be a man
> But not just any man—
> You could be Robert Mitchum
> Gregory Peck in *To Kill a Mockingbird*
> Gary Cooper in *Meet John Doe*
> Nick Nolte in *Who'll Stop the Rain*
> Jason Patric in *Rush*
> Lawrence of Stinking Arabia
> Jimmy Stewart in *Mr. Smith*
> Susan Sarandon in *Thelma and Louise*
> *A Man for All Seasons*
> *Saint Joan*
> Linda Fiorentino in *The Last Seduction*
> Linda Hamilton in *The Terminator*
> Linda Hunt in *Silverado*
> Linda Blair in *The Exorcist*

I wrote this poem fragment about Holly Hunter's talent about twenty years ago.

Her first starring role, in 1987's *Raising Arizona*, had left me unimpressed, but *Broadcast News*, released at Christmas the same year, knocked my socks off.

Holly Hunter was a force of nature, pure and simple.

The more I saw of her as her career progressed over the next decade, the more impressed I became.

You could be Griffin Dunne in *After Hours*
Or Roberto Begnini in *Down By Law*
Harpo Marx in *A Night at the Opera*
The nasty big teeth of Caerbannog
You could star in *Paris, Texas*
Take the title role in *Two Women*
Coil on a piano in *Baker Boys*
Replay Chris Walken's finest two minutes
You could be all those things
With Albert Einstein thrown in
(And you wouldn't be acting)
But I'd think no more of you than I do now

Because of the work I was doing in theater at the time, I was enamored of actresses who could inhabit and own male parts—because that's what Jenn did—and often envisioned Hunter playing other actors' career-defining roles.

The poem itself was a kind of catalog of many of my favorite films, and a riff on the gender-neutral power of Hunter's skills. Yes—she was gorgeous; but that was not what drew me to her performances. Instead, it was an intangible something, an energy that allowed her to go toe-to-toe with any co-star and more than hold her own.

It's not who you are
What you were before
Or even what you will be
It's not the things that you do
It's not the curve of your breast
Or the line of your thigh
It's not the slightest waist
Or the brownest eye

> It's what's just behind
> Something pure, and dangerous
> Silly, profound, strong and witty
> Something courageous, powerful and eternal

I found out today what that "something" was, thanks to the video archives we call *YouTube*.

During a Q&A session with acting students not long ago, Hunter was asked if she has a mantra or method of dealing with stress while working.

Hunter replied that, first, she doesn't allow negative emotion to surface while on the job. Instead, she pushes it inward with the expectation that the sublimated energy will be harnessed and find its way outward through the glee of performance, or other emotions that will positively feed and serve the character.

Second, said Hunter, she uses a mantra borrowed from Billie Jean King, who told her that "Champions adjust." So when things get bad, says Hunter, she tells herself, "I'm a champion. I'm a champion!"

Somewhere along the line, through my many musings about Hunter and her craft, I think I limned the source of her energy… and adapted it for my own life.

Long ago, when it seemed like the odds were stacked against me—whether it was at work, in relationships, or even while playing trivial games—I learned to tell myself, "Well, I always wanted to be legendary!" And I would push on through to the finish line, having faith in a miraculous comeback. And many times, it would happen.

In recent years, however, I've been learning (and seeing in the lives of those around me) that an identity of Champion or Legend comes not from confidence in self, even if it tends to manifest itself in that way; no. Ultimately, it comes from an underlying confidence in a universe that expects great things of us and wants us to cooperate with that grand vision.

It's not a matter of self-achievement. It's a matter of spiritual and psychological alignment. And it's beautiful to witness!

> Thrill your captive audience
> Screen it for me once more

■

Ginny Owens

I shared a wonderfully encouraging dinner with friends last night, and the timing was so good because my heart was heavy from a week of discouraging national news.

As if I needed any more conviction about our nation's hardness of heart, I listened to Ginny Owens' album *Something More* during my drive to dinner.

> My heart is heavy
> As I see what we've become
> How quickly we forget
> What we've been rescued from

These words are from the opening lines of "The Hand."

My ancestors, like yours, were all immigrants. Some came on the *Mayflower*... and no one questioned their need for asylum.

Some came as POW indentured servants; they knew what it meant to be held in detention indefinitely.

Some came from an impoverished and war-torn Europe at the end of the nineteenth century; for them, living in a sod house on a homestead in South Dakota was preferable to the hardships they had known "at home"... and they were lucky that they were Dutch, rather than Chinese, so that no one wanted to stop them at the border because they were "undesirable."

How quickly we forget what "our people" have been rescued from, and how like other people we really are.

How quickly we accept the compassion that both God and Man have shown to us, and then transform it into fear and contempt.

> If not for the Hand that leads us
> We, too, would roam in the darkness
> If not for the Hand that heals us
> We would live in pain

Hardness of heart isn't much to be wonderstruck about, is it? No. But I have more confidence in the power of compassion than I do in despair about the power of indifference. And not because *I* really do care, but because *God* really does care.

Do you?

> Our hands have power
> They can harm, and they can heal
> ...
> Won't we choose to use our hands
> To give the world His love

So, yeah... in spite of it all, I remain wonderstruck by the power and the appeal of compassion.

As I heard Billy Bob Thornton say the other day, "I'm proudest of what we just talked about: of kind of always knowing who I was. So that way I could just keep doing what I ought to be doing."

Take a look at yourself, and remember who you are.

Who your people really are. And then get about doing what you ought to be doing. Do the right thing.

Choose to use your hands to give the world—the whole world, and not just the people who look like you—a little love.

"During the valleys, you start dreaming again," says Thornton. "And I think that's one of the most important things you can do. ... Once you quit dreaming, it kills you."

■

Elvis Costello

Three things today about Elvis Costello.

Number One. I had already planned to write about Costello—but just as I sat down to write this note, I learned that he has cancelled upcoming tour dates in order to recover from an urgent cancer surgery. What an interesting coincidence.

It sounds, however, like he'll be just fine for the long haul and is encouraging other aging men not to ignore their scheduled cancer screenings. Good on him.

Number Two. I did not realize that Costello's 1980 recording of "I Stand Accused" was a cover of a song originally recorded by Tony Colton in 1965. How could this have escaped me all these years? I have always felt that the wordplay in the lyric was quintessential Costello and mentally cited it as an example of the "Costello style." Huh. This is simply something I should have known.

Number Three. Number Two aside, 1980's album *Get Happy* nonetheless includes many, many examples of the Costello style. I'll just deal with one here.

> Somewhere in the distance
> I can hear "Who Shot Sam?"

This is the cryptic opening line of "Motel Matches." But what the hell does it mean?

If one doesn't know that "Who Shot Sam?" is a song title, a listener can't even make grammatic sense of the sentence.

If one doesn't know about George Jones, even knowing that the lyric is a song title is of little help.

Further, if one doesn't know that the song is a George Jones Deep South tragedy, one can't appreciate the likely setting for the lyric's singer: some crappy motel on the road near Nashville or Texarkana, the kind of place with cheaply-printed books of matches in dingy glass ash trays.

These ten words, however, establish that Costello is the type of songwriter who *does* know "Who Shot Sam?", who *does* know all about George Jones, who understands quite well about living on the road and cheap motels and crappy ash trays… and about the people who use them. Perhaps someone just like him, or at least an unreasonable facsimile. Ten words to establish place and tone with his "establishing shot," much as a filmmaker does. Costello style: not just making music, but telling stories. Very telling stories.

> This is my conviction,
> that I am an innocent man

Typical Costello: taking a familiar phrase and turning it on its head by pairing it with another common phrase of contrasting or paradoxical conventional meaning. The hybrid produces thought of an entirely new kind. Costello is a lyricist who inhabits tarnished words and the mental world in which they whirl—and shine.

> I struck lucky with motel matches
> Falling for you without a second look
> Falling out of your open pocketbook
> Giving you away like motel matches

Also typical Costello: taking a metaphor and running with it. No, Costello isn't making love to sulphur on a cardboard stick; but isn't that a sultry metaphor for a one-night stand between a prostituted hook-writing traveling musician and a truck-stop hooker?

> I wake with the siren in an emergency

Yes, he wakes with the brazen siren at his side, almost certainly regretting his indiscretion; and the proverbial red lights are flashing, and the warning klaxons are sounding. Too much booze? Too much self-indulgence? Too little fidelity on the road, relational and audible? Yes, quite the disaster. Even if the wife at home never finds out. He knows, and that's bad enough.

> Though your mind is full of love
> In your eyes there is a vacancy

The warning signs are all there, upon reflection...

> And you know what I'll do
> When the light outside changes from red to blue

The writing is on the wall... and that's probably where this red-light romance started... "For a good time, call..." But when regret, or even common sense, or maybe sobriety, kicks in, the singer is back in George Jones territory, singing the blues about another wrong-headed fling gone south. And the girl winds up obviously worse for wear, tossed aside like a cheap matchbook filched from a dingy glass ashtray…

> Boys everywhere, fumbling with the catches
> I struck lucky with motel matches
> Falling for you without a second look
> Falling out of your open pocketbook
> Giving you away like motel matches

He knows he's not a man: no, still just a slowly aging adolescent journeyman relearning the mistakes of the rickety role models and broke-down singers gone before him.

I don't resonate much with Costello's world these days. But on occasion, as during this evening's drive, I can still be wonderstuck by his artistry.

And I can pray for his recovery.

∎

The Untouchables

Exactly thirty years ago, I was shooting *Who Shall Stand*, the sixty-minute Western I wrote and produced, in the Okanogan.

We filmed on weekends throughout the summer, loading up all the production gear about 3 AM on Saturday mornings and starting the five-hour drive to our primary Nighthawk location about 4:30. The caravan would travel via Blewett Pass, and each Saturday morning I would pop in my cassette tape of *The Good, the Bad and the Ugly* soundtrack as we approached Issaquah. If I timed it just right, and I usually did, "The Ecstasy of Gold" would be playing just as we crested Snoqualmie Pass.

I would then flip the cassette for *The Untouchables* soundtrack. Again, if I timed it right, the soaring melodies of the main theme would be playing as we flew over the top of Blewett Pass.

I was reminded of this as I made an early-morning trip to Twisp on Friday. I didn't have the timing quite right, but I did pretty much have Highway 97 to myself over Blewett as I blasted Ennio Morricone's score for the Brian De Palma film.

I saw *The Untouchables* on opening day, June 3, 1987, at the Uptown Theater with Shari Kooistra. The arresting title sequence of the film was designed not around filmed footage but graphics... and Morricone's music. I honestly cannot think of a film whose tone was better set in its opening seconds than was the theatrical release of *The Untouchables*. And that tone was: style.

De Palma does not specialize in verisimilitude. That is to say, he is not interested in presenting "reality" on film; he knows that the artform is one of calculated deception and manipulated point of view, and he embraces all of that via impressionist cinema.

In painting, impressionism is known for an emphasis on "depicting visual impressions of a moment" rather than a photo-like rendition of the moment itself; in music, "clarity of structure and theme is subordinate to harmonic effects, characteristically using the whole-tone scale"; in other arts, impressionism "seeks to capture a feeling or experience rather than to achieve accurate depiction."

You can see how these descriptions can easily apply to many films—even certain documentaries like those of Errol Morris or Michael Moore.

De Palma's approach to impressionism opts for heightened, stylized reality. He was aided in *The Untouchables* not only by Morricone's score but by David Mamet's brilliant, infinitely quotable script.

Mamet specializes in stylized, impressionist dialogue, and the overarching experience of *The Untouchables* is centered around the corrupting influence of the fight against evil: "I have foresworn myself," summarizes Elliot Ness; "I have broken every law I have sworn to uphold; I have become what I beheld and I am content that I have done right!"

This is not a sentiment we are intended to endorse, mind you; as with the central message of *Apocalypse Now!*, it's one that's meant to be sobering. Sometimes you gotta do what you gotta do, both films say, even if it would be horrific in other contexts. Unlike Francis Ford Coppola's grueling 1979 *tour de force*, however, De Palma's meditation on upping the ante is both High Art and superb pop entertainment.

In the mix are not only the genius of Morricone's Oscar-nominated score and Mamet's script, but the creative work of four brilliant actors. We need not say much about the legendary Sean Connery, who won an Oscar for his work here as Irish beat cop Jim Malone. But alongside him were three performers who would later become accomplished film directors in their own right: Kevin Costner, Charles Martin Smith, and Andy Garcia, each of whom delivered some of their best acting work here under De Palma.

Robert DeNiro was also pretty darned memorable as Al Capone. One notable scene follows the opening credits, as Capone hosts a press conference while getting a shave. De Palma's camera starts out directly overhead in a "God shot" as "the court" silently (and artificially) hangs on Capone's next words.

As the camera cranes down after establishing the shot, a reporter finally steps in to pose an obviously over-dubbed question: How is it that Capone, who runs Chicago, is not actually mayor?

The barber takes the hot towel from Capone's face, and Capone is both disturbed by the question and amused by it.

Today, one can't help but hear this indictment running through DeNiro's head: "Fake news!"

In Mamet's words from DeNiro's lips: "We laugh because it's funny, and we laugh because it's true." At the very least, we are entertained by Mamet's and De Palma's Chicago "because it's true" in a stylistic and moral sense, if not historically accurate.

The other of DeNiro's most memorable scenes is the vision of what "Keep Chicago Great" looks like, as he hosts a dinner for all his lieutenants in the wake of Eliott Ness's first liquor raid.

> A man becomes preeminent. He's expected to have enthusiasms. Enthusiasms, enthusiasms... What are mine? What draws my admiration? What is that which gives me joy? Baseball! A man stands alone at the plate. This is the time for what? For individual achievement. There he stands alone. But in the field, what? Part of a team. Teamwork... Looks, throws, catches, hustles. Part of one big team.

Standard big-business motivational speech. The kind of thing you might hear in the White House with the Cabinet.

> If his team don't field... what is he? You follow me? No one. Sunny day, the stands are full of fans. What does he have to say? I'm goin' out there for myself? But... I get nowhere unless the team wins.

Yeah, teamwork. And Capone proceeds to beat a man to death with a baseball bat, just so everyone gets the point about whose team they are all really on.

DeNiro's Capone is truly a cat who needs a comedown.

Hence Ness. Costner's transformation from the goodie-two-shoes crusader to jaded Treasury enforcer culminates at the courthouse during Capone's trial for tax evasion—one of the few historical details which the film gets "right" in its quest for a stylistic "impression" of the case of "The People vs. Al Capone."

In open court, it dawns on Ness that Capone henchman Frank Nitti is up to no good—and on a legal pretext, he has Nitti removed from court and searched, finding evidence that he was the trigger man behind Malone's murder. Nitti makes a break for it, and a chase ensues. When provoked, Ness ultimately throws Nitti from the roof of the courthouse rather than arrest him. (As we have noted, this is impressionist cinema, not realist.) Ness returns to the court and, with his memorable line about being content that he has "done right," proceeds to blackmail the presiding judge into switching juries with the courtroom next door.

Cue Capone's meltdown, and his attorney's resignation.

A very impressionistic conclusion. "Here endeth the lesson," indeed.

How *The Untouchables* ends up with only 8 out of 10 stars on IMDb and an 89% audience score on Rotten Tomatoes is beyond me. If you like Hollywood-style entertainment at all, you should find *The Untouchables* to die for.

But maybe it's too stylistically violent for many audiences; or, perhaps, it conveys too strong an impression of a certain truth: that we are all complicit in the evils that our world creates, either through the enthusiasms and appetites from which these evils arise, or through the levels to which we are willing to stoop to eradicate them.

I am wonderstruck by a great many things these days; and I guess maybe what I should say that what I was really wonderstruck by yesterday was nostalgia. Some works of art from back in the day never cease to fascinate me. And call me to something much better than sinking to the lowest common denominator!

■

Cris Krusen

The first formal film review I published was for *Final Solution* in 2003. The opening line of my review was: "*Final Solution* is about improbabilities."

At the time I reviewed the film, I was offered interviews with the producers, the stars, the real-life Gerrit Wolfaardt (who is the subject of the film), and the director—Cristóbal Krusen. I did not have my "sea legs" under me as a reviewer, however, so I did not want to be unduly influenced by the director (as I would be by Ridley Scott just a few years later while prepping my review of *Kingdom of Heaven*). So I declined to talk with Cris as part of that gig.

That fall, however, I happened to run into Cris at the Christian Booksellers Convention in Orlando, where my first book was being introduced by my publisher. Cris and I hit it off immediately.

I have stayed in touch with Cris ever since. Jenn and I published his book of prayer letters, *Let Me Have My Son*. I have consulted on several of Cris's scripts, including that of the award-winning *Sabina K.*, which I just reviewed last week. (Yes, I know—conflict of interest!)

The other evening, after a couple long days of yard work, a friend and I found ourselves at loose ends unexpectedly. Now, the two of us rarely choose to sit down and watch a movie—so the completely unlikely and spur-of-the-moment idea was: Greg, you pick a movie. We had just recently been discussing Cris's work, so I at first thought of suggesting *Sabina*; but something inside me said, No. *Final Solution*.

While my friend popped popcorn, I tried to find *Final Solution* online, but the usual Vimeo links were dead. I thought, "Well, I could call Cris and see if he could send me a link to something online." I initially dismissed the idea as silly. Nobody sits down to watch a movie by calling their director friends for private streaming links. But I called anyway!

"Hey, Cris. This is Greg. Really quick—I'm trying to find somewhere to stream *Final Solution*. But the Vimeo link is dead."

A momentary silence. Sort of stunned. "It so happens that I'm just now watching the final color corrections on the remastered film for the hi-def re-release. I'll email you the link. You'll have it in thirty seconds."

I walked back into the kitchen just as the popcorn was getting buttered. How bizarre is that? Wonderstruck.

Final Solution is about improbabilities. Paradoxically, it's also about realities. As presented in the story of Gerrit Wolfaardt, reality and improbability collide in the most natural of places—the soul.

■

Jake Gyllenhaal

Jake Gyllenhaal is of course a very surprising, memorable actor.

His first lead role as a teenager in *October Sky* made an indelible impression on audiences, and by his early twenties he was already a household name for roles in *Donnie Darko*, *The Day After Tomorrow*, *Brokeback Mountain*, and *Jarhead*. And it was so uncanny how much he looked like Evan Happel. Ha!

I was watching a Screen Actors Guild Foundation interview with Gyllenhaal last night, and he was asked if he ever felt like he had "owned" a role—if fate or destiny or the universe had simply intended him to play a certain role which he had "nailed."

Now, I've always felt that Gyllenhaal was a very thoughtful actor, but his response to the question nonetheless took me aback. He said "No"—because the nature of acting is ephemeral. That is, an acting "performance" is not something you accomplish; it's something you do and experience. It's not a thing to be "captured" and then admired or rejected.

Like many professional actors, Gyllenhaal does not watch his movies.

And he not only avoids critical reaction but also puts little stock in personal and fan reactions, which he says "can be easily misinterpreted."

"All we have as actors is the process," he explains. "I think we are mistaken when we think we have 'the result.'"

By this he means it's a mistake to judge the book by its back cover. You can't feel good about reaching the top of Everest if somebody carried you there; and if you've run the best race possible, it's immaterial if you won or lost. When it comes to acting, he says, "You read the screenplay, your read the play—you read whatever the words are—and then you have your experience [of those words], and hopefully you are moved by it. And hopefully you have the opportunity to do [the role]. And if you do do it, you'll never be able to see it. You give that up."

His wording here just floored me. I resonated with it, I suppose, as both an actor and director.

How striking. What a way to think about living. All we have are opportunities, chances to play a part in another person's life… and if we are blessed with the chance to play that role, and we take it, we voluntarily cede the right to understand the full impact of the role we will play. Because we *stop being spectators.*

We are a living impact, each step of the way. And all we have is the journey itself. In the end, "success" in relationships—in life itself—is not about achieving some desired end result. It's not ultimately goal-oriented. It's not about applause or awards.

"It's really not about the response," says Gyllenhaal. Because you can't own the role you have played; you can only do the best you can with how you have played your role. "It's about how you feel about it, no matter what."

We do well to invest in how we go about a thing rather than to focus on the end result. Satisfaction is certainly not about whether other people think you won or lost... or even about how they thought you played the game. All you have is your own integrity on the journey.

"I think somewhere that things are supposed to be a certain way, that I plan, I'm prepared," he goes on to say about how difficult it is to actually focus on the journey. "Preparation means so much to me. But I don't always trust that that preparation will lead me, that I can let go."

Gyllenhaal concludes:

> And that's that moment where you have to have faith. As an actor, so many elements will not be the way that you expect them to be. And when they are not, they are a blessing. Every single time they are a blessing. ... It's magic.

Find the magic in it all.

■

Warren Etheredge

I used to cross paths with Warren Etheredge quite a bit back in the day when I was regularly reviewing theatrical releases. Most often, we'd pass in the Seven Gables parking lot either before or after a screening, and we'd nod cordially.

I was still writing and editing for *HollywoodJesus.com*, and at the time Warren was producing *The Warren Report*, which specialized in filmmaker interviews. He would go on to found The Film School with Rick Stevenson, Tom Skerritt, and others, while I moved on to *Past the Popcorn...* and working with Rick on *The Best Films You've Never Seen* for Official Best of Fest.

I finally got to formally meet Warren a couple weeks ago and talk at length with him. Rick and a couple of colleagues operate The Prodigy Camp each year, bringing promising young filmmakers and musicians in from around the world for a week of intensive training and workshops. I dropped in for a couple days this year to audit workshops by Warren, Brian MacDonald, John Jacobsen, and others.

But Warren's workshop on story structure particularly floored me—a fact that I intended to write about but somehow never got around to. I was reminded of it this morning, though, when I opened up my journal to jot a note in reaction to some lines of poetry written by English poet Francis Thompson.

> Only in loss do you live the price of love.
> How brave are you?

And then I glanced up the page and saw my final note from Warren's workshop, when he said:

> The greatest conflict possible is the choice between two hopes.

That was such an arresting analysis of conflict dynamics in story structure—and in life. I reflected that we often want to boil things down to "wrong choice" vs. "right choice," as in the wholly unconflicted and dismal conclusion of Meg Ryan's choice in *Sleepless in Seattle*… when in reality, motives are usually more complicated than that.

Discerning which of two great things is actually the better, and which to choose… well, that's often a matter of perspective and point of view. And when you can't have both, disappointment and hurt are bound to follow for someone, no matter how great the hope that is chosen.

But that doesn't mean there is a villain in the story. It just means someone had some very hard choices to make.

We crave stories about hard choices.

We love stories about conflict, Warren says, because we find in them lessons for survival. By experiencing others' trials and choices vicariously, we get a leg up on how to address them in our own lives. That's from the audience point of view.

When speaking to writers, he tells them that "stories are the testing ground of our beliefs—which we don't really understand until they are tested."

I can honestly think of no higher human calling—for artists, or for anyone. What we believe shapes everything that we do. And since that's the case, we ought to be refining those beliefs with every spare bit of energy we have. Because eventually those beliefs will be tested.

And seriously: Don't you want to be equipped with the most battle-tested beliefs available when the time comes?

"Which beliefs," Warren asks his students, "are you willing to test?"

Which beliefs am I willing to test? I have been finding out.

How brave am I? We shall see.

As John Jacobsen advised in his workshop, "You must learn to be patient with your stories."

Sound familiar to anyone? Wonderstruck.

Yes, I am committed to the proposition that the universe wants us to be surprised, to be in awe of what comes next...

■

Keri Russell

Just five months ago, I wrote a pretty scathing review of Season 5 of FX's *The Americans*, calling the total effort "dull and rote."

Given that opinion, you may be surprised to learn that I decided to give Season 6, "The Final Season," a shot. Why? Perhaps because it's included with my Amazon Prime subscription.

Or maybe it was because of Keri Russell. Or maybe it was because of Jenn. Maybe it was both.

Twenty years ago, Jenn and I and a handful of other actors—Michael Brunk, Patty Cram, Lyla Moreland, George Rosok, Laura Inglis, Stefanie Kelly, Daryl Jones, Dave Stark—wrote three one-act plays about investigative agents in deep cover. The series may have been inspired by *The X-Files* and the biblical "Acts of the Apostles," but it sure looked and felt an awful lot like *The Americans*, in many ways.

As in *The Americans*, the scripts for *The Chi-Rho Files* were often quite dark. How could they not be? Passionate, driven agents leaving behind families and every shred of personal life in favor of a "greater good." You don't get to that promised land without sacrifice.

To culminate the series, I wrote my first full-length play, based on the characters and storyline that we had collectively created. *Homecoming* brought to a conclusion the story of Ana's search for her sister Perez, gone missing on assignment when Ana was just twelve years old. Twenty years down the line, and with Perez's former partner Nico—now Ana's handler—pushing her toward the conclusion of the mystery, the play both begins and concludes, in classic-flashback revelation, with Nico, Perez, and Ana all at gunpoint... Nico intent on salvaging his reputation, Ana intent on reclaiming her identity, Perez intent on living out her faith.

Early in the series, Perez was played by Jenn's sister Patty. For *Homecoming*, Perez was played alternately by Linda Woltz and Reba Jacobs. Jenn played Ana, and I played Nico.

Nico and Ana both face existential crises in the series finale, as do Elizabeth and Philip in the finale of *The Americans*. Which vision of the future wins out? The Old Way or the New Way?

In the Epilogue of *Homecoming*, I wrote the following lines for Jenn and me. I can still hear her voice foreshadowing her own fate in ways that we could not have imagined, as we delivered the last lines we would speak with our drama troupe. Jenn was not yet ill.

> Ana (VO, writing to Perez): What has happened here in Philadelphia has justified every belief. If I should die now, it will be with a certainty that my faith has been righteous. And if through death larger mysteries are revealed, I will have already learned the answer to the question that has driven me here. That there is a will in the universe greater than our own; that it was made flesh, and walked among us; that there are indeed true believers among us, and that nothing—

neither death, nor life, nor angels, nor principalities, nor things present, nor things to come, nor powers, nor height, nor depth, nor any other created thing—can prevail against them.

As she considers the lines she has written, there is a sound of approaching troops, rattling of locks and chains. The others stop humming and begin preparing themselves. Ana hurriedly folds her papers and stuffs them under the bunk's mattress. A figure behind Ana stirs, and rising, turns toward Ana.

Nico: Ana. Let's go home.

As I watched Keri Russell's performance in Season 6 of *The Americans*, I couldn't help but be floored at the emotional capital that Russell put into her character—and couldn't help but think of Jenn's parallel performance as Ana.

I couldn't help but think, *My God! Jenn could have played Elizabeth Jennings.*

I cannot help but be wonderstruck at what the crew at Dramatic Insights invested in each other at the turn of the century. And tonight, as the 19th anniversary of my marriage to Jenn draws to a close, I remain in awe of it all... knowing that Ana has indeed gone home... knowing that Tira—Ana's, and Jenn's, alter ego—has found peace... knowing that there is indeed a will in the universe greater than our own, and that there are true believers among us—true believers such as Jenn.

Peace. Peace be with you.

■

Jim Carrey

I am a sucker for interviews and documentary films about the creative process.

You may have noticed.

I have never been, however, much of a sucker for Jim Carrey. While I admit to being amused by much of Carrey's work, I do not find it drop-dead hilarious in the way that so many people obviously do. I suspect that I am overly sensitive to the deep pain that underlies much comedy, so I've never really warmed up to Carrey's super-intense approach to his work. Instead, when I watch Carrey perform I tend to think, "Wow. That dude has got some issues."

When *Man in the Moon* came out twenty years ago, however, I was pretty much right there ready to see what Miloš Forman and Carrey would do with their take on Andy Kaufman's equally over-the-top and troubled comedic work.

Jim and Andy were two nuts from the same shell, and in the hands of the Oscar-winning Forman the story was frightfully haunting. I don't think I would call the film brilliant or anything like that... but wow. It's been a hard one to get out of my head.

The other night I ran across *Jim and Andy: The Great Beyond*, a documentary released last year. Comprised of backstage footage shot during the filming of *Man in the Moon* plus brand-new interviews with Carrey talking about the experience, the documentary is nothing short of disturbing and illuminating. And challenging.

If you've paid any attention to the dramatic or film arts, you've probably heard about "method actors" sinking so deeply into their roles that the people they know must also live with the character for months at a time. Robert DeNiro and Daniel Day-Lewis, among others, are famous for this.

Well, Jim Carrey apparently took the cake with *Man in the Moon*. Not only did he "become" Kaufman for months while filming, he became the characters that Kaufman played. While Kaufman himself could fairly easily "come down" from his characters long enough to connect humanly with his collaborators (such as wrestler Jerry Lawler and writer Bob Zmuda), Carrey was so invested in the various roles that when the camera wasn't running, he rarely became even the "normal" Andy, much less the, um, normal Jim.

What transpired during filming made Joaquin Phoenix's very public "performance art" gig for the faux documentary *I'm Still Here* look like a petty party prank. Carrey reports that after he concluded filming on *Man in the Moon*, he literally had no idea who Jim Carrey was any more. He couldn't remember what he liked to do and had no idea what his politics were.

To run away from the "heartbreak" that he was experiencing, he so deeply buried himself in Andy Kaufman that he didn't—he *couldn't*—think about "Jim" for months.

Really truly scary stuff. And yet... Carrey digs out a gem of a silver lining at the end of the documentary. When reflecting on the common thread of "daddy issues" that he and Kaufman shared, Carrey notes that his own father's soul was worn down by pursuing a career that didn't fit him—and by getting tossed aside from that industry when he was only 51 years old. "I learned that you can fail at what you don't love," Carrey says. "So you might as well do what you love. There's really no choice to be made."

While this may seem like mere rationalization for Carrey's bizarre submersion into Kaufman's psyche, Carrey is onto something different.

"When you compromise," he explains, "and you fail, it really hurts. It hurts even more than failing at what you love."

I get this. I totally understand the antipathy for compromise. I am all in favor of going for the gusto when you find something you love. And I think Carrey really gets it, too. It's not just another elaborate put-on.

And he also gets that he probably took things too far with *Man in the Moon*. But again… how do you know what "too far" is if you don't give everything you've got? Once you compromise, you can be absolutely certain that you haven't gone far enough!

One thing of which Carrey is absolutely certain is the impact that his portrayal of Kaufman had.

And it's clear that he's spent some time thinking about the implication: He decided to be Andy Kaufman, in a way; and that choice, that full-tilt commitment, changed people's lives. It wasn't just a portrayal: It was an embodiment.

"Could I do that with other [historical] people?" Carrey muses.

"I wonder what would happen if I just decided to be Jesus?"

I wonder. I wonder indeed.

∎

Boadicea

Every once in a while I need an Enya fix. And when I do, I always look forward to the thrill of "Boadicea."

Jenn first immersed me in Enya's music twenty years ago. "New Age" was a genre I was aware of but had never really listened to. Those were waters in which Jenn swam, however, and the first track Jenn had me listen to was "Boadicea."

For those who don't know, Enya's music sometimes includes lyrical singing but often does entirely without words—just blends of instrument and voice... voice as instrument.

"Boadicea" is one of the songs in which Enya's voice is layered track upon track upon track, in this case producing a haunting effect of mood and emotion. It's a recording that never fails to amaze and move me.

Enya achieves with her music and voice what I strive for in poetry: establishment of an emotional setting over and above the specific mechanics of meter or rhythm or words or even meaning. Tone and general aesthetics most effectively open up the mind and heart to inspiration which transcends the intent of the artist—the best kind of art, in my book.

Enya wreaks this kind of musical magic better than any recording artist I know, except perhaps Roger Taylor (Queen's drummer, who has also released several solo LPs). Part of the effect that both singers can achieve is due to the unique characteristics of their voices—which, interestingly enough, span similarly wide vocal ranges. (Taylor's is D2-E6 while Enya's is B2-A5.) Their reedy voices lend themselves to sounding like instruments, and Enya in particular embraces the breathiness of her humming in ways that other recording artists typically avoid.

"Boadicea" is a song about the Celtic warrior queen Boudica (Latin name), who led a failed revolt against Roman occupation of Britain. Her forces slaughtered tens of thousands of Romans and Roman subjects, and sacked numerous Roman cities, including London. But Nero's legions ultimately prevailed and Boudica either died of illness or poisoned herself to avoid capture.

I don't think Enya's song captures any of that story… but who cares? What it does capture, regardless of its inspiration, is something stunning.

Look it up on YouTube or Pandora… and close your eyes and listen. I think you'll be transported to a different place and time.

■

Brian May

On my way home from my (final) weekly meeting with my friend Peter Alden last night, I decided to play Brian May's solo album *Back to the Light*, which I picked up while on a blizzard-interrupted business trip in Hartford, Connecticut, in February of 1993. (Less than a week later, I would be in Manhattan the day after the first World Trade Center bombing.)

Back to the Light was May's first solo disc issued in the wake of Freddie Mercury's death and the subsequent (premature) demise of Queen. The album opens with an eerie power-chord riff on the Christmas "Rocking Carol."

> Little Jesus, sweetly sleep, do not stir;
> We will lend a coat of fur.
> We will rock you, rock you, rock you
> We will rock you, rock you, rock you

Oh, yeah. A fascinating thing to listen to in the dead of night during a blizzard.

Did anyone else know that Queen's most famous lyric was cribbed from an ancient Christmas carol? I certainly didn't.

But this note isn't about *Back to the Light* in general, which is about rediscovery of purpose, passion, and vision.

Well... maybe it is.

Just before I reached home last night, the opening chords of "Resurrection" came over the speakers in my car.

> There's a pain in my brain
> Confusion in my heart
> ...
> Gonna make my resurrection
> No more of this crap
> Got a whole new direction
> Ain't no turning back
> Resurrection is a-gonna come

Yeah. There was no way I was going to just pull into my driveway in the middle of that kind of sentiment. And with the Yaris vibrating at full volume, I wasn't about to putter through Huntington Park's age 50+ community at 8:30 PM and rattle all the senior citizen windows.

So I cruised on down Marine View Drive to the abandoned Landmark on the Sound, one of my favorite places to watch a sunset die into the night. As Brian May sang and wailed on his guitar, I gazed out over the Sound across to the Olympic Mountains.

> There's no use in counting
> The price of those years
> There's too many heartaches
> And too many tears
> Gotta ride the night into the morning sun

Stopping at Landmark was a good choice. That was probably the last sunset I'll see from there before I move to Twisp next week and start the next chapter of my life.

For my birthday on Monday, old friend Michael Brunk and I watched a couple of documentaries about Queen's album *A Night at the Opera* and the making of "Bohemian Rhapsody."

At one point, while discussing his "Prophet's Song," Brian May talked about Queen's almost OCD drive to avoid repetition in their music.

> It was a very Queen thing. We liked to never repeat ourselves, even in the context of a song. We weren't one of these groups who would say, 'Oh, that's a nice chorus. We'll pop it in here, and here again.' There would never be that. You would always hear something different every time the chorus came around. It became a little trademark, I suppose. Something that really keeps you on your toes internally, as well—always looking for new colors. And the new colors sometimes relate to the words; maybe there's a new point to be made in the next chorus, because the song has moved on.
>
> You know, songs, to me, are journeys. And if you find yourself repeating a chorus, maybe there isn't much of a journey to the song.

Just yeah. Oh, very, very yeah. There's a metaphor for how to live, eh? Resurrection is a-gonna come.

And when you are resurrected, it's to new life—not the same old thing. Says May,

> There is no way that you can ever really repeat something. I have this great belief that the magic of the moment can never be recaptured.

■

Queen

The circumstances under which I first listened to *A Night at the Opera* were quite unique.

In December of 1975 my brother, Bob, was dating Linda Stanford, whose family was old friends of ours from the years we spent in Missouri in the 1960s. Linda's little brother Bob and I were great chums as well, so I was pretty tight with the Stanford family.

On the Saturday night before Christmas that year, Linda gave me a wrapped gift—and it was obvious that it was an album. That night, I was staying with my sister, Elane, at a house she was sitting for a friend, and I took that gift with me. In the morning, we rose early enough to have a lot of spare time before heading for church—so I opened my gift from Linda to see what it was: Queen's *A Night at the Opera*, which had been released in late November.

"Bohemian Rhapsody" had been playing on the radio for several weeks already. But I did not know anybody who had purchased the album. Elane and I decided to give it a spin before we headed out.

Once we started, we couldn't possibly stop. From the opening number, "Death on Two Legs (Dedicated to...)," it was very clear that we were listening to an album unlike anything we had heard before.

Musically, the album is all over the map—in a brilliantly orchestrated way. Guitar-driven screeds, old-fashioned novelty tunes, blues jams, romantic ballads, 12-string sci-fi stories, epic apocalyptic visions, and, of course, "Bohemian Rhapsody." To call the album eclectic is to be understated; and the wide-ranging musicianship required to pull off every genre and style is simply astonishing. Even Queen detractors agree that their studio albums from 1975, 1976, and 1977 display unparalleled musical skill. The production values were literally ground-breaking.

At thirteen years old, all I knew was that the ideas of "pop music" or "rock and roll" were never going to be the same again. I had no clue what half of these songs were "about" or what all these wildly varied musical concepts signified; but I sure wanted to find out. This was an artistic world I craved to explore. And I think I did, in my own lost and confused fashion.

Fast forward to 2006: Classic Albums released the 100-minute documentary *Queen: The Making of A Night at the Opera*. I accidentally ran across the DVD at a now-defunct record shop on Queen Anne Avenue in Seattle. After watching it while Jenn fought off a blossoming sleep disorder known as narcolepsy, I spent the next decade plotting a special birthday celebration for myself—a combo listening/watching party: focused listen-through of the album, followed by the DVD and a bonus of the brilliant 2004 BBC special about the making of "Bohemian Rhapsody."

As I have mentioned previously, Michael Brunk was game for finally making this mini-party happen this year. On Labor Day, we donned headphones, and I queued up the gold-plated

Original Master Recording CD that Mark Stevens bought me for Christmas in 1992. After 45 rapturously engaging minutes, Mike and I cracked open a superb bottle of handcrafted hard cider that Elane bought for my birthday, tore open a bag of gourmet salt and malt vinegar chips, and spun the DVD.

By the time we got to the closing segment of the Richard E. Grant-narrated BBC doc on YouTube, I was in heaven. The over-the-top and archly counterpointed analysis of the meaning of "Bohemian Rhapsody" had me clutching myself with hilarity and delight. I have not laughed like that in a very, very, very long time. What a gift.

What a series of gifts. What joy.

What an album. What a day. What a privilege. What a treasured life the universe has provided for me.

As I was flying back from Nashville a year ago, just ten days after Jenn had made the decision to go on hospice care, I listened to Queen's first six albums back to back.

Upon reflection at the end of that flight, after forty-some years, it finally dawned on me what the appeal of their early music has been for me all these years: the irrepressible romanticism of it, in the formal sense, and an undeniable, optimistic belief in goodness and beauty. A determination, almost, that some delightful surprise is around every corner. That even mistakes or tragedies can be grand, glorious, and legendary. Beautiful.

Because of what comes next.

I believe that today. Oh, do I believe it.

Oh, do I need to believe it.

Just before Mike left on Monday night, he said, "You know, there's one more observation I ought to make. I don't often listen to an album straight through the way we did; but as we did I was struck by how much your life has been like *A Night at the Opera*, Greg. I think this album had more of an influence on your life than you know."

Mike may be right. He just may be.

And you know what? That makes me smile. Because now I think I know what's behind the penultimate line of "Bohemian Rhapsody."

It's irony.

Because *everything* matters to me. Everything.

Thank you, Freddie.

■

Kevin Costner

I first saw Kevin Costner in *Silverado* when it opened on July 9, 1985.

And what revelations that film and his performance were! He was by no means an unknown entity to me, however, as his role as Alex in *The Big Chill* had been talked about in film industry mags for a couple of years.

You don't remember seeing Costner in *The Big Chill*, you say? You would be correct, because no one did. Alex is the dead friend that everyone in *The Big Chill* talks about, but all of Costner's flashback scenes were (legendarily) cut from the final film by director Lawrence Kasdan.

To make up for the cut, however, Kasdan wrote the role of Jake in *Silverado* specifically for Costner. And what a memorable—and career-defining—role it was. A pretty astounding speaking-role debut.

(I will note that, sadly, Costner's performance as Jake was also about the most energetic of Costner's career. In interviews, he has often remarked that the character of Jake is about as far from his real-life personality that he has ever played. It shows, and not in a particularly good way! He should probably get outside himself more often when he works.)

I watched an extended interview with Costner via the Screen Actors Guild Foundation the other day and found out a great deal of surprising information about his career. Unlike a great many screen actors, Costner is not the product of a life-long ambition or strategic plan for success. Rather, Costner is more the product of "you don't know what you don't know" serendipity. That is, he has attempted bold things in his career and life simply because he hasn't known enough to be intimidated.

In the absence of facts and experience, one can only be so pragmatic. I could say a great deal about this, but instead of blathering on about it I will just close with Costner's own remarks, which are plenty insightful enough.

"Some people give me credit for being very, very brave there," he says in reference to casting the late Whitney Houston in *The Bodyguard* (yet another collaboration with Kasdan). "And I'm thinking I almost don't understand what people mean: 'That was a brave choice, that was a brave thing.' I'm thinking to myself, 'This is what I wanted to do.'"

■

Bill Paxton

Whenever I move, the first things I get sorted out are music and movies. Even if the rest of the house isn't settled, I want to be able to rock out while I unpack and end the day with a little couch time.

This time around, I test-drove my new home-entertainment setup with *One False Move*, director Carl Franklin's stunning little film of Billy Bob Thornton's screenwriting debut about a two-bit hood (Thornton) on a tragic collision course with small-town sheriff Dale "Hurricane" Dixon (Bill Paxton). Along the way, collateral damage stacks up like pleasure boats after Hurricane Sandy.

This 1992 film was not only "made" by Siskel and Ebert's championing, it also cemented the film critics' reputation as America's Only Critics You Could Actually Trust.

It's a hard film to watch. Thornton's Ray and Michael Beach's chilling Pluto are truly pieces of work on an amoral bender, and the racial politics of the film—involving both Black Lives Matter-style abuses of White power and the subtext that director Franklin is himself African American—were simultaneously way ahead of and behind its time, oddly and sadly. Layer on the deadly tragedy at the core of the film, and this is not what one would call "a popcorn film."

But at every level, *One False Move* is about as close to "truth" as cinema gets. Every brutal or poignant note feels genuine, and at the heart of it all is the apropos-of-everything force of nature that is/was Dale Dixon and Bill Paxton.

Just about the whole world heard about his sudden death at 61 years old last year, a post-surgery stroke claiming his life in the wake of attempts to correct childhood heart damage. I could read tributes and obits to and about Paxton all day. They remind me of the many, many memorable roles from Paxton's career: the endlessly quotable Private Hudson in *Aliens*; *Apollo 13*; *Twister*, in his first true "leading man" role opposite Helen Hunt; his gripping reunion with Thornton in Sam Raimi's *A Simple Plan*; and his absolutely deranged self-directing debut in *Frailty*... among others.

But *One False Move* will always be the quintessential Paxton performance. The emotional crux of the film comes not in a hail of bullets—though the stylistic tension that Franklin ratchets up in the leadup to the final shootout is truly an epic *tour de force* of directorial and editorial technique—but in a quiet cafe scene where Hurricane overhears his big-city counterparts laughing at Dale's small-town over-ambitious buffoonery.

From this point on, Paxton's performance "goes small" and the "interior work" that he does absolutely shines through in a masterwork of subtlety and pathos. As violent and ugly as this film is, it is also one of the most beautiful portraits of human selflessness I have ever seen. I count myself as a pacifist by and large, one who nonetheless recognizes the hypocritical paradoxes involved in adopting a non-violent position in a relentlessly violent world; and by the time the bloodbath is over at the film's conclusion, David Mamet's line from *The Untouchables* never fails to come to mind in a fully justified fashion: "I have become what I beheld, and I am content that I have done right."

This world is tragically broken, and it claims good souls like Dale Dixon—and Bill Paxton—all the time.

"Game over," Bill. And you played it very, very well.

■

Nathan Clark George

I first became aware of Nathan Clark George's music when I was sent a review copy of *Pull Up a Chair*, a DVD/CD combo of a live performance of George's music.

My March 2009 review of the DVD was titled, "Music from Eden," an apt description. "George's music easily earns much more than a casual listen," I wrote at the time. "There's something instantly arresting about it; his string-and-percussion quartet arrangements seem grander, somehow, than ordinary folk music—and anyone with much knowledge of Scripture at all will soon recognize a good deal of George's lyrics."

Before long, I had purchased every track of George's music I could find and have followed him since. His music was a staple for both Jenn and me, and its gentle, convicting spirituality has been an enormous factor in my personal growth—and ability to find wonder in the world.

I was fortunate enough to run into George and his wonderful, patient wife at a conference in Nashville exactly one year ago and spend twenty minutes talking with them about George's art. He graciously answered questions that Jenn and I had had about various songs and lyrics, and treated me more as a peer than as a wonderstruck fan. I now count him among my friends.

As I left my new home in Twisp Saturday morning for a long morning drive to the Olympic Peninsula, I came into Pateros just as the sunrise was painting the sky and the final bend of the Methow River with glorious splashes of red. I was listening to George's *Pull Up a Chair* as I drove, and "Fuller Sense of Place" was playing.

> I'm not a native
> But I love it here
> You can tell from the smile that's on my face
> I'm not a native
> But I love it here
> And I believe I've found a fuller sense of place
>
> Out here where the grass bends east
> The winds drive your soul
> For so long now
> I've tried my best
> To find a home
> And watch now as the prairie rolls
> And settles in your eyes
> See how life can slow
> And peace take your mind
> Clouds rise and storm this field
> And lights dance on my face
> The pouring rains have driven me to you
> In faith
>
> I'm not a native
> But I love it here
> You can tell from the smile that's on my face
> I'm not a native

> But I love it here
> And I believe I've found a fuller sense of place
> Yes, I believe I've found a fuller sense of place
> Yes, I believe

I have listened to that song wistfully for years, feeling in my soul that yearning for a fuller sense of place—for a fuller sense of grace.

For most of my adult life I have felt like an alien in the places I have lived; but as I left home on Saturday and drove down the Methow, I finally felt like I was leaving a place I loved—a place I didn't want to leave.

I have learned so much this year about myself and my place in the world. I am so grateful for it all.

You can tell from the smile that's on my face.

■

Hill and Stone

No, I'm not talking about nature this time.

Well, maybe I am. I'm talking about Jonah Hill and Emma Stone, who both stepped out to executive-produce the Netflix original series *Maniac*, which debuted a couple weeks ago. The series itself, which is kind of a neo-steampunk sci-fi tale of pharma love (if that makes any sense at all, which it shouldn't), is pretty darned decent—if full enough of dark, violent humor that it's not really an "all-ages" or "Safe for the Whole Sainted Enclave" sort of entertainment. Just sayin'.

But I'm not wonderstruck by Stone and Hill because they made a decent TV series... or because the sound of their names goes down so nicely, regardless of the order in which you put Hill and Stone. (How's that for egalitarian?) I'm really in awe because of the characters these actors backed with their own resources.

Typically, actors executive produce so they can a.) have some measure of control over the product; and b.) look good, mostly. But the mind-bending, soul-healing script for *Maniac* has Hill playing about the most emotionless, inertia-saddled, depressed guy you'll ever spend nine or ten hours watching. And oddly, you can't *stop* watching. Yes, in "dream sequences," Hill gets to loosen up quite a bit—but still: I am impressed that Hill chose this role for himself. It's not an actor's dream—it's a part designed to kick an actor's backside.

Kudos, bro. You stepped up, and you nailed it.

Likewise, Emma Stone picked a part that has her looking bad all the time. Well, not *all* the time. Again, because she's Emma Stone and because of those dream sequences, Stone gets to look all kinds of good, too—even dynamite. But still: watching Stone in *Maniac* is kind of the cinema equivalent of the post-honeymoon phase, or living together. Aside from the dye job, you get to see what Stone looks like in just about every phase of life. And while I wouldn't call that "brave"—because soldiers and mothers are brave, not artists—I will call it a "bold" and "surprising" choice.

"We talked about mental health and neuroses more than I ever really have at work before," Stone told *The Star*.

> It was something we all cared very much about, being sensitive and compassionate in telling a story that is about radical self-acceptance and connection.
>
> Nobody is completely "normal"; I don't think anybody really understands what normal is.

The compassion really comes through in this program, as does the meaning of real friendship. "I was so focused on my own shit," Stone's Annie says in an apologetic speech she has prepared for Hill's Owen. "I should have said I care about you. And that after everything we've been through, I can't *not* have you in my life. It's actually really hard to just connect with somebody. When you do, you don't—you *can't*—just run away."

At least, not separately. It's also a nice touch that Annie never gets to deliver this speech to Owen.

Thank you, Hill and Stone, for an exceedingly natural love story.

Stone continues:

> Grief follows you—it gets easier, sort of, but it's always a weight on you. That's the insane part of being human, that we have to lose each other and hurt each other. So it's comforting to explore that unifying feeling that happens in pain and know that it's just a part of the human experience.

■

Henry Poole

> For while we were still helpless, at the appointed moment, Christ died for the ungodly.

That's a quote from the Bible.

Is that offensive? Is my invocation of Scripture and Christ backward and unenlightened? Is the concept of "the ungodly" not only passé but bigoted?

How about the very notion of "the appointed moment"? Isn't that something relegated to fairy tales and wishful thinking? Isn't the idea that everything—and I mean *everything*—happens for a reason one for which there is no rational defense?

After all, if God meant for you to meet your future spouse at a particular place and time, then he must also have meant for that sheet of plywood to come flying out of that pickup truck bed and slash through your niece's windshield, killing her instantly.

Right? You can't cherry-pick Providence.

Let's face it. A purposeful universe can be terribly inconvenient, brutal, and hard to explain.

But here's the deal. Everything in my experience points to that conclusion.

And you, dear reader, should *above anyone else* agree with me.

Why? Because you most likely enjoy movies.

Follow along with me, and I'll explain, starting first with my conclusion, then working backward toward your fascination with film, and wrapping up with some thoughts on the film *Henry Poole Is Here*. Because that's what got me thinking about all of this.

So this is my conclusion: 9/11 was not meaningless.

That ISIS beheaded a certain twelve people instead of a different twelve is not random or without purpose. It's not entirely incidental that the Patriots won Super Bowl XLIX rather than the Seahawks. It matters that I once ran into Lorraine Bergen Drake or Karen Evans at Bartell, rather than Scott Schaefer or Michael Brunk. There simply are no accidents.

I have not come to this conclusion lightly or without reservations. After all, if absolutely *everything* has a point, then every word I speak or write should be carefully considered. My slightest action could promulgate a butterfly-effect disaster—or love fest—on the other side of the world.

The notion also potentially makes me the victim of every whim of every friend, neighbor, and stranger... let alone those who would intend to harm me, or the proclivity of the Earth to belch forth lava or wipe out 200,000 people at a time with tsunamis.

And it begs me to account for Hurricane Katrina, Nazi Germany, and chlorine gas.

It's hard enough to say these things can be construed to have a positive purpose. It's harder yet to say, "Yes—and there's a God who not only lets these things happen, but has a plan that incorporates all of them."

But try denying that everything which has happened previously has conspired to bring us, quite exactly, to where we are today. And if *any* good comes of that, then the precedent "bad" was not only sufficient but *necessary*.

Chesterton was on to something when he said that the things we call "bad" are simply good things that are not good enough to satisfy us. We just don't have the luxury of seeing the Big Picture, what filmmakers call "the God shot."

But I've certainly seen the difficult truth of this global, "macro" paradox work itself out on the "micro" level in my own life. I was bullied for years as a child and was addicted to pornography by the time I was twelve years old. As a coping mechanism for my exceedingly ungodly struggles, I developed an alternate persona that I didn't even discover existed until I was thirty-six—the night of October 9, 1998, exactly twenty years ago.

But all of that played together to make me the ideal mate for my equally flawed and troubled wife. Further, we wouldn't have traded the final years of Jenn's chronic, life-threatening illness for anything because through that suffering, not in spite of it, we learned the greatest spiritual truths of our lives.

Would it have been nice if things had played out differently, at least at certain points? Perhaps. But I really don't know what the full implications of those theoretically minor changes might be. All I really can be certain of is my limited perception of where I happen to be in the current arc of my story.

I still struggle, and in other ungodly ways if no longer with pornography. And it's hard to accept that I am not the author of my own story, much less its hero.

Certain wide-release movies like *The Truman Show* and *Stranger Than Fiction* have explored these ideas in some limited fashion. The first time I personally ran up against them in art was my first read through *The Lord of the Rings*. When I reached the Bridge of Khazad-dûm, I went right into the abyss with Gandalf and the Balrog. How could Tolkien have killed off Gandalf? What was the point of reading any further? I literally threw the book down in disgust. But I knew...

I knew there were still hundreds of pages left to read and that there were, in fact, *two full books* remaining in the trilogy. Tolkien *had a reason*. There was more to the story, and I had to find out what that was. I picked the book back up, and I was not disappointed.

When I discovered films like *Sorcerer* and *Apocalypse Now!*—directors like Friedkin, Coppola, Carroll Ballard, Cimino, Peter Hyams, even Woody Allen—I realized that I had a thirst for art that made sense out of the universe... that I almost literally *craved* an artform which, by definition and conception, demonstrated that everything—literally everything—mattered.

And this is where you come in. I think you have that craving, too.

And that you have it, rooted deep down, whether you profess that everything has purpose and meaning, or whether you rebel against the notion with every fiber of your intellect, "kicking at the goads," if you will. Because even the most ardent atheists I know love films—and not the films of *avante-garde artistes* which reflect in method and theme a random, purposeless view of the cosmos (and those do exist) but exquisitely crafted, purposeful films like *Fury Road, Lawrence of Arabia, Apocalypse Now!, Platoon,* or *Rob Roy*.

Or, perhaps, *Henry Poole Is Here*, which elevates the dialogue to a whole new plane because it not only exhibits this exquisite level of craft, but because, thematically, it is explicitly about purpose, meaning, and even faith.

At every level imaginable, Henry Poole lives a frustrated life. He is getting nothing he wants, having to settle for second, third, or last-best in every area of his life. Shortly after he moves into his new home, in which it would be generous to say he lives, his neighbor Esperanza believes she has found the face of Christ manifest in a rust stain on Henry's exterior wall.

When the stain appears to bleed, and miracles appear to happen for those who believe it's a manifestation of Jesus, Esperanza wants to call in the Catholic Church to officially enshrine Henry's wall. Henry wants nothing of the kind. He just wants to be left alone.

Or does he?

That's the narrative tension which provides the backbone of this film, a thoughtful, funny, and entertaining exploration of philosophy in which every character name, every line of dialogue, every soundtrack choice, every shot composition and POV has bearing on the film's direction and meaning.

Filmmaking, in case you haven't noticed, is exceedingly purposeful.

Now, here's the really odd thing. When this film was originally released in 2008, Jenn and I were editing and managing two film-review sites, *Hollywood Jesus* and *Past the Popcorn*. Between the two sites, we had a staff of some thirty reviewers. On the day *Henry Poole* hit theaters, we published fifteen or more different reviews—and two of them were for *Henry Poole*. My own personal assignment that week was an interview with director Gil Cates, Jr., who had just released his small film *Deal* direct to home video. So I didn't see *Henry Poole* at that time.

Then it disappeared from theaters so fast I didn't see it at all. When it came out on home video, I received an unsolicited screener. Because it wasn't on my editorial calendar and because we'd already covered it for both PtP and HJ, I simply filed the screener and didn't give it a second thought.

Over the years I would periodically leaf through my screener library and think, "I'm gonna have to watch that someday." But someday never came.

Not long ago, I leafed through my screener library and once again ran across *Henry Poole Is Here*. And I said, "I think I have just the movie for today."

It was a Sunday morning, and as was often the case, Jenn hadn't been physically capable of leaving the house for church.

We weren't even through the credits before it was evident that Poole was not just spiritually minded—it was spiritually *saturated*. And again, the dilemma that Henry Poole confronts is: What are you going to do when it appears that Jesus is crying tears of blood on your wall?

And there is a moment of decision in the film where Henry literally reaches out to Jesus. Will he accept the invitation and put his finger in the wound, figuratively speaking, or will he turn away?

And could you believe it? Just at that precise moment, just as the singer on the soundtrack pronounced the word "joy"— the DVD player *froze*.

There was Henry on the big screen, caught in this eternal moment of decision, caught hanging forever between joy and the void. And no amount of pausing or playing was going to fix it. There was no button to push to get Henry out of his predicament, to prompt Henry toward one decision or the other. If there were any one second out of the 7000 during that film you'd call the crux, this was it. And the DVD player froze.

I was dumbstruck.

This has never happened with my DVD player before or since.

Was the DVD defective? Would I be able to find out how Henry's story ended?

Did it matter?

Was it simply more significant that the moment of crisis came at all?

Was it sufficient to know that the filmmaker had a purpose for Henry, whether I knew it or not?

Well, my curiosity got the better of me. After all, could I have lived without finishing *The Lord of the Rings*?

I pulled the power on the DVD player, plugged it back in, and restarted the movie. I then jumped to the closing credits just to confirm that the DVD actually *had* more scenes on it. Then I cut back to the scene where the DVD stalled. Would it get stuck there again? Would I be able to finish the movie? As hard as I tried, I couldn't get the DVD player to freeze again.

There is absolutely *no technical reason* for that DVD to have gotten stuck where it did when it did.

How could something so absolutely random happen with such precise timing, stretching out over a series of events years long, culminating in a particular, very specific instant?

From my point of view, this was not random. Henry Poole and his moment of decision had been sent to me at just the right time—at a very specific, appointed time.

I believe that everything happens for a reason.

And for me, *Henry Poole* is not just here. It's a miracle.

■

Skybound Blue

I wouldn't have listened to the album *Better Than the Plans We Made* last night if things had gone my way.

What an irony.

Hell, I didn't even realize that was the title of the album when I put it on. I didn't look at it that closely.

I saw husband/wife duo Jenny and Matt Behnke perform at the Brewminatti Block Party in Prosser on Labor Day Weekend—part of a personal birthday celebration that *also* did not go exactly as I had planned. Skybound Blue only got to perform a 45-minute set, but I was taken enough with what I heard to be convinced that I needed to hear more—so I bought a couple of their CDs, without so much as looking at them, and stuffed them in my camera bag for a rainy day.

Well, yesterday was far from a rainy day at Ocean Shores— but things rarely work out the way that we expect. I was here, a CD player was handy, and I had my gear bag with me for the first time in several weeks. I remembered the Skybound Blue CDs and popped in one of them. The second song on the CD was the title track... and boy, did it catch my attention.

> It's better than the plans we made
> Every broken dream, I wouldn't trade
> Because it's better than the plans we made

"Best to shoot for the moon," Jenny sings, "if you want to hit the stars," echoing a mountaineering metaphor to which I have long adhered. Getting to Camp IV on the standard route to the top of Everest is no small accomplishment—but if you're not aiming for the top of the mountain, the odds of getting to Camp IV are about nil.

Here's a fact: The vast majority of things do not go exactly the way that we intend. But I firmly believe that every "failure," every detour, every interruption, every disappointment in life points us to something different—which, if we are open to it, can be "better than the plans we made."

Perhaps collaborative artists appreciate this idea of "happy accidents" a little better than most folks—but my primary professional background is in project management and engineering. While I have experienced the deep satisfaction of a four-year multi-million-dollar project fulfilling the original specification, I also believe that the energy one puts into trying to tame the universe is not generally rewarded.

Perhaps I was just not cut out for that life—but "I can do all things through the strength of my own will and talents" is a road that is bound to end in deep disappointment. A plan is just a framework on which to hang God's surprises.

Go ahead, make a plan. Make a ton of them!

And then prepare to be awed by what *actually* happens.

■

The New World

"The gift that keeps on giving" was a slogan used by Kodak (and others) for many, many years.

I generally feel that way about music and about Antonín Leopold Dvořák's Symphony #9, *From the New World*, in particular.

Not long ago, Michael Brunk told me that he thought Queen's 1975 album *A Night at the Opera* had influenced my life in more ways than I suspected. He is probably right, as my junior-high years established a great many of my musical preferences and tastes—and shaped the way that I perceived myself and my place in the world.

The same is undoubtedly true of Dvořák's symphony. At the same time as I was discovering Queen, I was also discovering orchestral music. I had started playing alto saxophone in fifth grade. At eight years old, when presented with a list of instruments from which I could choose, I read the word "saxophone" and thought "bagpipes."

Get it? "Sax" = "sacks" = "sack" = "bag"? Yes, I was a sharp cookie.

I was so pleased that my mom said "yes" to saxophone and so disappointed to find out what a saxophone actually *was*. Alas! My mom told it me it was just as well, since I would have had to practice bagpipes out in the woods.

The band director at Showalter Junior High, Rodger Pinkley, was a super cool guy. He had a hot, hot temper and could get beet red with apoplectic rage; but the anger was never directed at specific kids nor expressed in a destructive way. (Says the guy with his own anger issues.) But he was always pushing the concert band (and stage band) to get better and better and better.

The climax of this ambition came in my 9th-grade year when he selected the fourth movement of Dvořák's Symphony #9 as the showpiece for the spring concert. What an aggressive, visionary choice for a smallish band of junior highers! The amazing thing is that we actually did the piece justice. Our French hornist, Mary Van Hee, in particular practiced her butt off for that performance.

When I started practicing the music at home, I discovered that my dad had LPs of several Dvořák symphonies, and a love affair began. The Czech composer's music has been a staple of my library ever since. While I was in college, I discovered an audiophile recording of German conductor Herbert Von Karajan conducting Dvořák's 9th with the Berlin Philharmonic, and I swear I was in Nirvana. (Before that band was a band.)

The symphonic form appeals to me for many of same reasons that Queen's music has always appealed to me: It is grandiose, theatrical, and demanding. A symphony will run anywhere from thirty-five to sixty minutes and requires you to take time out from life to "sit with it a spell."

Dvořák's Symphony #9 particularly appeals to me because I studied it in order to play it, and because it is so well-thought-out and controlled in its composition. Dvořák makes particularly good use of timpani, French horns, and the low strings. I also deeply associate *From the New World* with my own discovery of the wonders of the American wilderness.

In my teens and early twenties, I was simultaneously devouring orchestral music and exploring the peaks and rivers of the Cascades. The musical themes of Dvořák's Symphony #9 simply go well with a love of the outdoors. After I saw my first IMAX film in 1978—*To Fly*, at the Smithsonian—I began thinking of what an IMAX story set to *From the New World* might look like. Those images have been percolating in my brain for forty years now.

In December 2010, I had some time to kill at London's Heathrow airport, and I ran into Adrian Wyard. I was in town to cover the Royal Premiere of *The Voyage of the Dawn Treader*. Adrian was home visiting his mother.

I had become acquainted with Adrian via Dick Staub's podcast *Kindlings Muse*, for which Adrian and I were sometime guests. Adrian is a visual artist, technologist, theoretician, philanthropist, and raconteur.

As you might imagine, we had no lack of things to talk about while we waited for different flights in London. Shortly afterward, we began a collaboration for some years on the Tyee Photography Alliance. My first (exceedingly brief) Wonderstruck note, in April this year, was about the experience I had at the Auburn Symphony, a performance which featured Adrian's visual arrangements to Holst's *The Planets*. At the time, I learned that Adrian had also authored a visual accompaniment to Dvorak's *New World* symphony.

When I learned that I would actually be in town for a performance of Adrian's visual arrangement of *#9* at Seattle's Benaroya Hall the other night, I was elated!

I really appreciated Anthony Spain's direction of the Northwest Symphony Orchestra for this piece. In the years since I first discovered Von Karajan's "authoritative" interpretation of the symphony, I have gradually come to feel that he rushed it, so that it feels more like Wagner than Beethoven. Apparently Spain agrees, lingering over the opening of the first movement and the entirety of the second—which was especially languid and lovely with the lunar imagery that Adrian selected for that section.

What an absolute delight the evening was, as the program included not only Dvořák's Symphony #9 but "America the Beautiful" with massed choir, a new composition titled "Forestia," a piece from Wagner, and a performance by The Musical Mountaineers. I attended the concert with my Grand Canyon companion Max Losee, and connected afterward with longtime family friends Gwendolyn Koch and her daughters Elizabeth Gillihan and Reba Jacobs. Both music and the outdoors have formed the basis of my long friendship with the Koch family! I helped guide Reba and Elizabeth on their first backpacking trip, in the Alpine Lakes Wilderness.

I also enjoyed the opportunity to speak briefly with Mr. Spain about his interpretation of the symphony.

Sometimes a night at the symphony is just a night at the symphony; sometimes it is lushly sums up forty years of life.

And when that happens… wow. Look out.

■

Church of the Beloved

> Do not be afraid to question your God.
> He is not afraid.
> It's what he wants for you
> to grow in knowledge of him,
> for you to know that you can trust.

I became aware of Church of the Beloved in Edmonds via a theology school classmate, Lynda Homan. I had met much of her large family, which had extended greatly needed grace and hospitality to me in times of need, a fairly radical brand of hospitality that grew out of their American Orthodox faith.

Lynda's daughter Lacey Brown, a brilliant percussionist and musician, had begun living in community with Church of the Beloved and contributed to the community's first album of worship music, *Hope for a Tree Cut Down*. Even the title of the album, taken from the biblical book of Job, is crazy and provocative.

I was immediately taken by it.

A dozen years ago, when the album was first released, the idea of the Church as God's Beloved was still novel to me. I was not personally confronted by my failure to envision my own self as beloved by God until my sojourn with Christian Formation & Direction Ministries Northwest from 2012 to 2014. And not until this year have I finally accepted that God really *does* love me, and wants me to know and feel that love in a compelling and tangible way.

What a journey it has been. And one fueled by so much doubt. So much healthy doubt.

Ryan Marsh was the "Beloved Architect" of the Church of the Beloved, an outgrowth of a Lutheran prayer initiative. I have never managed to visit myself and yet have been greatly impacted from afar—not just via Lacey and Lynda, nor just via Tara Ward's lyrics, but through the entire aesthetic that Church of the Beloved exudes.

Faith—well, my faith, anyway—needs to be challenged, needs the example of those who are willing to pursue radical peace, radical love, radical commitment, and radical doubt. While I, myself, may not be called to such specific radicalism, I do need consistent reminding that my own tendency is to retreat from the edge, to be more spectator than actor. (This may be hard to believe even for those of you who know me well—but it's nonetheless true.)

This is a typical invitation to communion at Church of the Beloved:

> The table of Jesus is your place of gathering. Here you are welcomed, wanted, loved. Here there is a place set for you. So come all you who thirst and hunger for life. All you whose souls cry out for healing. All you who are weighed down with worry. All you who go hungry in a fat land. All you who search for meaning, or belonging but cannot find it. Jesus invites you.
>
> Draw near and trust that God is with you.

These words are expressive of a vision that steps outside the comfort of our usual patterns of welcome, of congregating based on natural affinities and convenient tribalism—and yet hopeful of finding a greater, grander peace in discomfort. I continue to be fed and encouraged by that vision.

Yesterday, I particularly needed to hear the words of "Do Not Be Afraid":

> Do not be afraid to ask for what you need.
> Do not be afraid to fall apart and free.
> You just might get what you asked for
> and you may find out who you are.

The universe is not afraid of your doubt. It is more powerful and eternal than your fear. And it wants so much more for you than you could possibly ask or imagine.

Ask for what you need.

You just might get what you asked for, and you may find out who you are. There can be nothing better.

■

Glenn Miller

I remember the day that Big Band music hooked me.

I remember it like it was today. Which is to say, I might not remember it that well at all, given that I'm now fifty-six and prone to "senior moments." Ha!

Anyhoo... When I arrived at Showalter Junior High, I attended a "welcome" pep rally in the gymnasium. For "warm-up" music, the junior high "stage band" was performing. I was, yes, wonderstruck. Until that moment, I did not know such a thing existed.

Sure, I was enrolled in concert band, just like any good nerd would be... but this? *This?*

This is what I wanted to do. I simply knew it. And decided it right that moment.

What I didn't know was the music the band was playing: Count Basie, Duke Ellington, Glenn Miller. All were completely foreign to me.

I also didn't know how to get into Stage Band. I soon asked around, though, and discovered that you had to get As in concert band, or something like that, and you had to be an 8th grader.

Oh, my, was 7th grade a loooong year.

I also didn't know that choosing alto sax in 5th grade was about as fortuitous a choice as possible for my Stage Band goal (and in a way that the bagpipes never would have been). As the only alto saxophonist in my grade, I was a near lock for inclusion in the band… and would be, if I did not screw things up, in line for the sax section lead in my 9th grade year. When I discovered this, it was about enough to make this band nerd pee his pants. Oh, my.

Well, I did not screw it up. This was the first dream of my life to come true. And part of that dream was discovery of the richness of Glenn Miller's music.

For those who don't know, Miller's band stood out from the pack of 1930s and early 1940s Big Bands because of his unique orchestrations. As a struggling bandleader, he struck on the idea of having the melody lead most often doubled on clarinet and alto sax. Not only were melodies thus stronger than with other bands, the blending of these two reeds offered a distinct sound. The rest, as they say, was history.

My own history with Stage Band continued through my sophomore year in high school. There, tenor saxophonist Randy Sartin and I were reunited with junior saxophonists Michael Veldman and David Palmer on tenor and alto, along with bari saxophonist Tim Byam. Under Dave's leadership and Mike's suave musicianship, that was one tight, tight unit. The rest of that award-winning band, especially Paul Wagner on piano, was equally strong.

The highlight of the year was playing a six-hour dance for the National Science Teachers Association at the Olympic Hotel in Seattle. Divine.

I bailed at the end of that year because I couldn't stomach the politics of concert band under conductor Greg Goss's manipulative misleadership… but I never forgot the love of Big Band swing. With the advent of the digital age, I was finally able to find (and afford) a complete set of every recording that Glenn Miller's band ever made. Whenever I want to, I can listen to Miller's music for nine hours straight without repeating a tune.

And when I want to, being *able* to is sheer delight.

Earlier this year, I was doing a lot of driving, for hours and hours over several weeks. While doing so I was indulging heavily in Miller's music. And while indulging, I realized one reason Miller's music has always appealed to me so strongly. The music is full of joy and is unabashedly romantic. Some might say even sappily so.

Kind of like me. And I'm not apologizing.

While I was in the middle of this Miller joy-binge, my *Past the Popcorn* colleague Jeff Walls posted up a link to his Seattle Film Institute project *Life Ain't No Musical*. This short film features a young man, not so very unlike Jeff himself, who approaches every day—and every "scene" of every day—as if it's part of a Hollywood musical.

While I've never seen Jeff actually break into song as he enters a room, his film protagonist does… and suffers the scorn of strangers, fans, and his girl.

The film climaxes with Jeff's alter-ego in moonlight on his balcony singing along to "I've Gotta Be Me."

> Whether I'm right or whether I'm wrong
> Whether I find a place in this world or never belong
> I gotta be me, I've gotta be me
> What else can I be but what I am

I've been rediscovering who I am this year, thanks to the support of those I love and those who love me. And yeah… I'm rediscovering that I am one mushy sentimentalist.

So be it!

> I'll go it alone, that's how it must be
> I can't be right for somebody else
> If I'm not right for me
> I gotta be free, I've gotta be free
> Daring to try, to do it or die
> I've gotta be me

Thanks, Glenn—and you, too, Jeff!—for daring to be different, for being boldly you.

■

Sway Wild

I would be incorrect in stating that I first saw Sway Wild—Dave McGraw and Mandy Fer—at the Brewminatti Block Party in Prosser on Labor Day Weekend.

That's because I was set up at the stage at the *opposite* end of the block to see Freddy & Francine perform, as they were my main reason for being at the Block Party. I would be correct, however, in saying that I first *heard* Sway Wild perform there and that I first saw guitarist Fer do her magical thing when she joined F&F on stage for a few songs.

Saturday night, Sway Wild, based on San Juan Island, played a gig at Copper Glance in Winthrop as part of a "two-night tour" of Eastern Washington. Oh... and the show was free, fully subsidized by the venue's owners. Copper Glance's performance space is just 600 square feet—so there were only about forty people squeezed in on a frosty autumn night, and I had a bar-stool seat literally within arm's reach of the band. And Sway Wild played for three hours. Yeah. Sweet.

I'd be hard pressed to nail down what really struck me about this encounter, however. The energy and dynamism that Fer and McGraw, and bassist Thomas Lord, put into that performance was just... well, something else.

I intend to say little about the music, because I'd really rather you *hear* what Sway Wild does with Lord's and McGraw's rhythm section while Fer leads on vocals and electric guitar.

But the Sway Wild trio is a relatively new configuration for the band, and they have not yet recorded definitive versions of many of their songs.

One, which Fer told me goes by the temporary name of "Ramstack," runs probably eight minutes or more live, with an impressive extended blues/funk jam in the middle. It really knocked me out. Also particularly riveting was an electric-guitar version of one of their older tunes, "Trainwreck," a hurtling instrumental with no lyrics whatsoever. I doubt that they will re-record that for their first Sway Wild sessions next month, so it was real treat hearing Fer shred on that to close the first set.

I was also taken by a song that I presume is entitled "Enough," though I can't place it in their recorded repertoire. Based on an "n of two," as mathematicians would say, I have the impression that Sway Wild is still finding its groove while being perilously close to crystallizing.

This intimate performance was far more energetic and electric than the 45-minute set they were able to bring to Prosser as a foursome a mere eight weeks ago.

At Copper Glance, I witnessed rare artistry—as when I first saw Freddy & Francine at St. Andrew's House in January or The Stray Cats at the Eagles Hippodrome during their first full U.S. tour in 1982. McGraw and Fer blend well on their vocals, and Fer is brilliantly engaging to front the trio. Their songwriting is intelligent and thought-provoking as well; but the real spark is McGraw, Fer, and Lord simply jamming. I could watch them perform all night… and almost did!

They closed their show, as they did in Prosser, with a sweet rendition of Fleetwood Mac's "Dreams."

> Play the way you feel it
> But listen carefully to the sound
> Of your loneliness
> Like a heartbeat drives you mad
> In the stillness of remembering what you had
> And what you lost, and what you had, and what you lost

It's a curious choice for an encore. I've always read the song as a downer, about as negative a heartbreaking take on dreams as you can get. Sway Wild, by contrast, seems to me to be all about energy, and hope, and looking forward.

I look forward to seeing them perform again, and hearing their first recordings as Sway Wild.

And I'm glad to be connected to them by the length of Highway 20.

■

Free Solo

So this is the ordinary reason to be dumbfounded by Alex Honnold: In June of 2017, the 32-year-old Honnold climbed the entire 3000-foot face of Yosemite's El Capitan in just three hours and 56 minutes.

Without ropes, aid, or support.

With camera crews watching.

This unreal feat is the subject of the excellent film *Free Solo* (the name for the genre of climbing that Honnold favors), which I was fortunate to catch at Winthrop's wonderful Barnyard Cinema.

But the climb and the movie are not really what strike me about Honnold. What fascinates me the most is his focus on what is most important in his life and his ability to keep "secondary" issues in perspective.

Note that I put *secondary* in quotes. This convention means that I am using the word ironically.

I am fairly certain that most people would not recommend considering a partner or spouse a secondary concern, as Honnold does. I also imagine that very few people could abide living in a van for years on end simply because of a desire to live close to their place of occupation/vocation. Honnold's focus on climbing also borders on the obsessive…

but how could it not be, when, to do what Honnold does, he must memorize an endless series of moves and then execute them all without a single mistake?

Imagine, for instance, doing a one-man show of the entire text of *Hamlet* (which runs nearly four hours), playing all the parts yourself, and knowing that if you flubbed a single line or entrance you'd be executed. Yes, I think you'd be pretty obsessive about getting your part down pat.

Which begs the question: Why choose a pastime that requires such obsessive attention to detail?

The film explains part of the answer to that question for Honnold, which is that his brain doesn't function the way that most people's brains do. His amygdala simply needs one helluva lot more stimulation than does yours or mine in order to light up.

Another part of the answer is one that runs through all of adventure, climbing, and mountaineering literature: Surviving in extreme environments simply makes certain people feel more alive and helps them navigate "real life" more sanely.

But what about those "secondary" concerns and where they intersect in "real life"? It's pretty clear that for girlfriend Sanni McCandless, and friends like Jimmy Chin or Tommy Caldwell, Honnold's *primary* concern is a pretty hard thing to stand by and watch.

Still, the appeal of being around a person like Honnold is obvious. Such single-minded devotion reminds us how passionless most of our lives are, and by contrast reminds us of what vitality can look like. And it's frankly kind of hilarious to see priorities put in their proper place.

When Honnold and McCandless go shopping for a refrigerator for Honnold's first home, he is thrilled almost beyond words to find an actual basic icebox free of gizmos, gadgets, and stainless steel. He lovingly describes the basic white appliance as "so adequate!"

Refreshing, and hilarious.

■

Francis Thompson

"Yes, Greg," said the universe to me. "You were meant to have these poems."

I suppose I feel this way in part because I feel that way about the universe in general... but is that such a bad thing? I think not. If I thought it were, I wouldn't be writing Wonderstruck.

Nonetheless: How the poems of Victorian English poet Francis Thompson found their way to me is pretty unlikely.

That Thompson's poems were published in the first place is improbable. A sickly, failed medical student, Thompson was, by the age of twenty-nine, homeless, near death, and addicted to opium. He was essentially what we would consider today as an indigent drug addict of the sort swarming the streets of Seattle. But he walked the same London streets and alleys as Jack the Ripper and the Ripper's victims. He even knew a couple of the victims, intimately.

He was also a talented poet rescued from the streets by patrons of the arts who happened to be publishers.

The rest is literary history, as the Meynells arranged for Thompson's treatment and rehab, and published his works—the most famous of which is "The Hound of Heaven."

If you have not heard the poem itself, you have almost certainly heard pop-culture references to the poem, even if you did not realize it or remember it.

Which brings me back to the present day. On August 16, I met Andrew Townsend in Vancouver, B.C.

To be perfectly honest, I didn't want to be there. That was probably the roughest week of the year for me, emotionally, and I was in the middle of prep for my move to Twisp.

My history with Andrew is also rather odd. A native resident of Manchester, England, Andrew became a fan of the *Lord of the Rings* coverage at *Hollywood Jesus*. When I delivered a paper at the Tolkien 2005 celebration at Birmingham's Aston University, Andrew brought his boys along to meet Jenn and me.

The day that I was scheduled to deliver my paper, Andrew led the five of us on an impromptu walking tour of Birmingham, which didn't work out so well for Jenn, as ill as she was—and especially so after a cloudburst caught us all unawares. Not exactly the best way to prepare for a presentation.

Over the next couple of years, Andrew contributed a dynamite series of articles about *The Hobbit* to *Hollywood Jesus*, and when he brought his family to visit relatives in British Columbia in 2010, we arranged to meet in Port Townsend, Washington. Between longer-than-anticipated travel times and ferry schedules, Andrew was significantly delayed, and I recall that we ended up with only a few minutes to chat before I had to return to Seattle for a meeting. Another disappointing day with Andrew.

So I was not exactly anticipating the best of luck connecting with Andrew on August 16 this year. The track record decidedly suggested otherwise.

But the rendezvous went off without a hitch, and we ended up with nearly the whole day to catch up thoroughly and enjoyably.

And then I received perhaps the strangest gift ever. Andrew and I have the shared experience of having "left the fold" of believers in our twenties and then returning to faith because the alternatives weren't particularly working. Andrew said that, for him, the experience was much like that described in "The Hound of Heaven."

I couldn't say that I agreed, because I had never read the poem.

And then Andrew produced a 1911 edition of *Selected Poems* by Francis Thompson. He had purchased it at The Sanctuary in Lyme Regis, the bookstore featured in *The French Lieutenant's Woman.*

Lyme Regis also played a key role in J.R.R. Tolkien's life, as his family stayed there on summer holidays.

"I'd like you to have this," Andrew said. "I purchased it for someone else, but I won't be seeing him on this trip."

I was second in line for a second-hand gift.

Nice.

But it made sense for Andrew, and for our friendship. And, apparently, for the universe.

I started into the volume during my Labor Day weekend trip to Prosser, digesting Thompson's work slowly, like one does with good wine or good cheese, as part of my morning meditations. I left the volume at home when I went to Europe, however, not wanting to lose or damage it during my travels.

I did not hit "The Hound of Heaven" until my return.

> My freshness spent its wavering shower i' the dust;
> And now my heart is as a broken fount,
> Wherein tear-drippings stagnate, spilt down ever
> From the dank thoughts that shiver
> Upon the sighful branches of my mind.
> Such is; what is to be?
> The pulp so bitter, how shall taste the rind?

Okay—so Thompson's arch Victorianese ain't gonna be to everyone's taste.

But… yeah. That snippet expresses about how I felt on August 16, when Andrew backhanded me that gift. Not because of Andrew, or the manner of the gift, but because of those other places I would rather have been.

But "The Hound" does also indeed express the promise on which Andrew and I have lived:

> All which I took from thee
> I did but take,
> Not for thy harms,
> But just that thou might'st seek it in My arms.
> All which thy child's mistake
> Fancies as lost, I have stored for thee at home:
> Rise, clasp My hand, and come!

God does pursue us with love and diligence.

I confess that while Thompson's language is rich, the subject matter of his early work is often pedantic and tedious. But good Lord! When his powers reached their full maturity in epic lyrical works such as "A Corymbus for Autumn" or "The Mistress of Vision," excerpted below, Thompson's work evokes the greatest of anything that Shakespeare ever wrote.

> Pierce thy heart to find the key;
> With thee take
> Only what none else would keep;
> Learn to dream when thou dost wake,
> Learn to wake when thou dost sleep.
> Learn to water joy with tears,
> Learn from fears to vanquish fears;
> To hope, for thou dar'st not despair,
> Exult, for that thou dar'st not grieve;
> Plough thou the rock until it bear;
> Know, for thou else couldst not believe;
> Lose, that the lost thou may'st receive;
> Die, for none other way canst live.
> When earth and heaven lay down their veil,
> And that apocalypse turns thee pale;
> When thy seeing blindeth thee
> To what thy fellow-mortals see;
> When their sight to thee is sightless;
> Their living, death; their light, most lightless;
> Search no more—
> Pass the gates of Luthany, tread the region Elenore.

Gives me chills every time I read that.

But what, pray tell, are Luthany and Elenore? Tolkien—a disciple of Thompson, and writing in his wake—could tell you, as I discovered. Luthany was one of Tolkien's early names for his land of Luthien, a mythological stand-in for the "sundered lands" of England. By contrast, Elanor was a flower of Middle-earth descended from Tol Eressea in the West, the gateway to Valinor. The flower's name means "sun star" in Tolkien's Elvish.

Quoting extensively from the Master's thesis of George F. Carter:

> To the perceptive reader, the use of the names "Luthany" and "Elenore" are not accidental or arbitrary; indeed, they provide the "key." The correlation of "Luthany" with the "key" lies in the fact that it is personifying and Anglicizing the Greek aorist, passive, infinitive of luo, which is luthenai, and means "to be broken." The correlation of "Elenore" with the "key" lies in the fact that it is an Anglicization of the Latinization of the Greek word meaning, "light," hellen, roughly a form of the name by which the Greeks called themselves. It also means "illumination." Thus, the reading of the last line of the quotation above would be: "Pass through the gates where you are broken, then tread the region of the land of Light"; or, "To him that overcometh, to him will I give to eat of the tree of life, which is in the Paradise of God."

Revelation, anyone?

The passage of Frodo into the West at the end of *The Lord of the Rings* represents a living passage into Paradise of one who endured great suffering in this broken world—something that both Thompson and Tolkien knew a great deal about.

Not at all coincidental that Thompson's life ambition should appeal to Tolkien. That my lifelong dance with Tolkien should come full circle this year in a return to the roots of Tolkien's inspiration, and in such a roundabout and literary way, astounds me.

I am dumbstruck… or would be, if it weren't for my capacity with words.

> To be the poet of the return to nature is somewhat, but I would be the poet of the return to God. ~Francis Thompson

■

The Lord of the Rings

August 20, 2017, Glenferness, Morayshire.

Just before we left home for this visit to Scotland, Jenn confessed that she can, at this point, barely tolerate anything associated with the *Lord of the Rings* films. (I can hardly blame her; I only recently re-acquired my admiration and enjoyment of them after ten years of *Hobbit*-induced disgust and loathing.)

The one exception, she said, is the soundtrack for *The Return of the King*. "Everything else about the films," she explained, "leaves me in knots. It's all tension with no resolution." But the *Return* soundtrack? "There's closure. Howard Shore did an amazing job of writing a score that takes you on a journey but leaves you someplace new. I have to *finish* the soundtrack, though, if I start. If I stop anywhere else, I'm left with that tension."

It's a pretty brilliant bit of insight, I told her, and one that Howard Shore would love to hear. He had the advantage, of course, that the third film had a real ending (several of them, and too many, critics argue), but Shore's score is indeed masterful, destined to be one of the great pieces of 21st-century music. It captures what Tolkien called the "eucatastrophe," the turning of darkness to sudden joy… and more, really: the entire scope of Tolkien's theory of "Escape, Recovery, and Consolation."

I'm feeling very little of that trinity this morning—no eucatastrophic joy at all. I'm awake long before I want to be and can't get back to sleep.

After reading a bit, I head out for a long walk.

During our 2005 visit to Glenferness, I am reminded as I head toward the ancient Princess Stone on the banks of the Findhorn River, Jenn was also very weak. It wasn't until the last day of that trip that she mustered the energy for the very same walk I am taking this morning.

As we returned from that walk in 2005, I shot the footage which I used to open the video I created for her after rafting the Grand Canyon in 2006. "This is your life," Jon Foreman sings; "are you who you want to be?"

As I recall that walk this morning, all I can do is cry.

I don't want to go home. I don't want to go home at all.

I don't want to leave knowing that I will likely never walk this path with Jenn again. In many ways, she already feels gone.

I could say so much about *The Lord of the Rings*. That's not surprising, given that I have written two books on the subject and lectured extensively here and abroad. Aside from the Bible, there is no work of literature I have studied so much.

Yet this is what I want to tell you.

This morning I finished a draft of three novellas by friend and librarian Loren Rosson III. They are generational sequels to the Netflix series *Stranger Things*, and Loren's final volume revolves significantly around a screening of Peter Jackson's films. To say more would be spoilers, should you ever have the opportunity to read Loren's fan fiction.

But it is so fitting that I should read those chapters, today of all days, as I recall the closing chapters of another great story—one that I actually lived.

And so fitting that Loren finds such similar inspiration from J.R.R. Tolkien's words, Peter Jackson's images, and Howard Shore's music.

> June 11, 2017, Des Moines, Washington.
>
> This morning I tell Jenn about some thoughts I've had regarding Peter Jackson's *The Return of the King*.
>
> When the film was released in 2004, both David Stark and I agreed that Jackson's portrayal of Samwise Gamgee and Frodo Baggins bore a great deal of resemblance to our friendship... only neither of us could really figure out, between us, who was Sam and who was Frodo.
>
> After some reflection over the last couple of days, I tell Jenn, I have a hard time believing how much has changed in thirteen years. There's no doubt that she and I are now far more like Sam and Frodo than Dave and I ever were. And it's clear who's Frodo and who's Sam. "I can't carry it for you, Mr. Frodo. But I can carry you!"
>
> I would give anything to be able to take Jenn's burdens away.
>
> And yet, as she has often observed, Sam's role is really harder than Frodo's. Jackson captured that so well.

Tomorrow, November 22, 2018, will mark the anniversary of Jenn's death. The following day, I have plans to attend a day-long marathon of *The Lord of the Rings* Extended Editions with John and Angie Prince and friends.

What strange bookending of an even stranger Thanksgiving.

August 21, 2017, Glenferness.

At 8:00 PM, just a couple of hours before we head to Aberdeen for our flight back to Seattle, I suggest to Jenn that we walk down to the Princess Stone. Jenn agrees.

I drive us down to the pheasant field to get us as close as possible, and we walk slowly down the trail hand in hand. In the gloaming we come to the Stone.

"Let's not say it's the last time," Jenn murmurs.

I agree. No "last times around" for us. Ever.

Jenn's already got her work cut out to make it back up the hill from the Stone, so we opt out of continuing down to the Findhorn. We are in no rush getting back to the car.

It feels good to take our time with those 300 yards. It feels very good.

At 11:30 PM we're out the door for our midnight drive, saying goodbye to the Studio, saying goodbye to Glenferness.

As we head out the drive, a red deer jumps out across the road. We say goodbye to it, too. But not forever.

Outside of time, at the very least, we will always walk the trails along the Findhorn.

∎

Winterlings

> don't forget the sacred skin on which you stand

Remarkable.

I was chowing down on ribs at The Methow Valley Ciderhouse, which was the real agenda for the evening, when I caught that lyric rumbling from the throat of Wolff Bowden, half of The Winterlings.

I really hadn't shown up for the music, but the music sure showed up for me.

According to the bio on the band's website (which just might be a myth... but does it matter?),

> Wolff grew up in a house on stilts, fifteen feet above a Florida swamp. Summer brought symphonies of alligators, owls and frogs. But in Wolff's recurring dream, it was always winter, and he stood beside a bonfire, singing to half-animal, half-human beings he called Winterlings. Two decades later, the Winterlings had come to symbolize life's deepest callings—the voices that beckon dreamers from the highway to the woods. He listened to the Winterlings and began painting for ten hours at a time, covering canvases with otherworldly beings.

The next step for Wolff was to connect with Amanda at a "Buddhist fire ritual" and be immersed in writing words and music "from the depths of the American wilderness."

The following morning at Winthrop Friendship Alliance Church, I listened to pastor Jason Suter preach about the power of "dangerous" faith, and I couldn't help but think of The Winterlings. Yeah, they're out there—but you don't get from here to somewhere else without first going "out there." And it's the artists who very often blaze the trail for us, if we are willing to let these brave souls do so on our behalf... and if we are convinced that where we are is not enough.

Think of that lyric again, from their new song tentatively titled, "Gonna Rise."

> don't forget the sacred skin on which you stand

Yeah. The sacred skin on which you stand. It's yours. It is in your soles.

Where are you going to place your next step? Where is that path going to lead you? What holy surprise does the universe hold in store for you? Don't just crouch there and cower. Start moving. Blessed are the feet of those who bring good news.

"This is the distance between you and me," sang Wolff in "If I Were Away," another in a series of masterful songs I heard that night. "How many footsteps more do I need?"

> If I was a radio, I'd tune this song for you
> about the things I might have been in worlds we never knew
> If I was a record I would spin and spin and spin
> cause time is just a needle on this skin I'm living in

Jon Foreman once said about Switchfoot's album *Hello Hurricane* that the band wanted to record a whole album of songs that they'd be happy to die playing. This is the kind of passion that drives The Winterlings.

> If I was a river I would flow right through your life
> and wash away the darkness like the day erases night
> If I was a house I would hold back heavy snow
> and keep your books and blankets warm each time you go
> If I was a dancer I would cross this open stage
> and if I was away, I'd come back to you someday

That sacred skin takes us places we never, ever thought we'd go, doesn't it?

I leaned against a door jamb and wept as I listened.

> If I was a breath, I would fill your empty chest
> with all the wind that I could fit inside my fishing net
> If I was a fire I would burn right through this wind
> And let you know the kind of smoke and ash I'm living in
> If I was a poet I would know just what to say
> and if I was away, I'd come back to you someday

Oh, if only I were a poet. If only.

■

Billy Knapp

Mr. Arthur had no idea what he would say to Billy Knapp.

The phone rang, so I put *The Ballad of Buster Scruggs* on pause and got up to answer.

I had just scrawled the following words from the dialogue of "The Girl Who Got Rattled," the fifth story anthologized by the Coens' *Ballad* on Netflix.

Down the ages of the past, what certainties survive?

As I made my way to the phone, I chuckled. What certainties, indeed? Even down through my fifty-six years, what certainties survive?

Of this only am I sure, I thought. *I have passed from one curious incubator to the next.*

I sat down at the computer to answer the phone. Naturally, it was a spam call. I chuckled again, and then I looked at my computer. My Facebook notifications screen was up, and it was reminding me that I ought to write. Ought to write.

Ought? Ought I really? No, I ought not. I will write when it makes sense to write.

Writing is not an obligation. It is a response to what moves me. I am moved often enough. I need not move myself. The universe has me well in hand.

I have been passed to a new, very curious incubator. Something will hatch soon enough.

I returned to the couch—and to the tale of Alice Longabaugh and William Knapp.

Mr. Knapp is a guide on the Oregon Trail. He has been partnered with Mr. Arthur for twelve years—an easy partnership, and a steady (if nearly wordless), but Billy Knapp has come to the age when he foresees two ways before him: settling down and raising kids who will care for him when he is old, or never doing so.

Miss Longabaugh has lost her domineering brother to TB on the Trail. As a kept sister, she has no idea how to manage her affairs or future. Mr. Knapp has a proposal for her. One evening, they talk over Alice's cookfire.

This is an awfully tender tale for the Coen Brothers and for *The Ballad of Buster Scruggs*. The script for this segment is also incredibly well written.

"Uncertainty," muses Billy. "That is appropriate for matters of this world. Only regarding the next do we vouchsafe certainty."

The words from this reserved master of the Great Plains reach Alice's heart and draw her in.

> I believe certainty regarding that which we can see and touch—it is seldom justified, if ever. Down the ages from our remote past, what certainties survive? And yet we hurry to fashion new ones, wanting their comfort.

I am floored. The false comfort of vain certainties.

Didn't I just write about "the sacred skin on which we stand" a couple of days ago? Didn't The Winterlings move me to write, "Where are you going to place your next step? Where is that path going to lead you? What holy surprise does the universe hold in store for you?" Were not those words inspired by yet another unlooked-for and wondrous day?

"What you know is contained in an old battered shoe box," I jotted yesterday as I mused about my own incubators.

> What you don't know is everything else.
>
> The rules that you have about what's knowable—and how you go about the very knowing of things—came to you from within your box. If you want to know what's outside the box, it's time to throw away those severely constrained rules—rules designed by someone else to keep you safe from the dangers (and the wonders) of what's outside your box.

I did not expect to find my thoughts echoed back to me today through the cinema of the Coen brothers. I did not expect to be moved as I rose from my desk in the wake of a junk phone call.

But I never expect certainty.

Certainty... Huh! That's the easy path.

■

Ajeet Kaur

> Walk quietly my love
> Let's kiss this earth we walk upon
> With our steps

I think the last thing I expected to run across at the TwispWorks "Gear Up for the Holidays" event last week was the art and music of Ajeet Kaur.

Then again, I don't know why I should have been surprised. I am consistently awestruck by this place. I can hardly walk out my door without being astounded.

And that night, in addition to wonderful artists I have previously met—like Kelleigh McMillan, Hannah Viano, Laura Gunnip, Sara Ashford, and Sherry Malotte—I had already enjoyed stimulating conversations with Craig and Perri Howard, Patrick Hannigan, Paul Gitchos, and Rod Weagant.

Then I wandered into Lesa Sevin's workspace upstairs from Confluence Gallery.

> What is the sound
> Of the song in your heart
> Listen Close

Lesa runs Marigold School of the Arts, "integrating creativity, imagination, and the natural world." The school "offers opportunities for people of all ages to explore ideas, take action, and experience transformational growth" while Lesa herself pursues dye- and paint-centric art in paper and fabric media.

I introduced myself to her by stepping on one of her pieces of art. Ouch!

As I toured her workspace and enjoyed her art, we talked of common interests—and then I spied a piece of craftpaper upon which Lesa had copied that opening stanza of "La Luna": "Walk quietly my love / Let's kiss this earth we walk upon / With our steps."

My heart about stopped. Those words were so in tune with the week that I had already been having and would continue to have. Lesa told me about the song "La Luna" and about Ajeet Kaur, the artist who recorded it.

> Dance wildly my love
> Let's throw our songs into the wind
> And let them echo echo

As focused as I was that night on the local community and the artists with whom I talked, the universe also reached into me from far outside and moved me tremendously. I am so grateful for that serendipitous encounter and for Lesa's gentle soul, availability, and relational generosity of spirit.

Yes, the dark night was cold—but it was also so very, very warm. "Winter is coming" may be one way to filter experience and deal with the future; but so may "spring is coming." As Kaur writes on her website,

Starting to feel the tingle of Spring waking up. Slowly unfurling like a fern to the sun, rising from this deep creative healing time of winter. Feeling a much more connected time of sharing with you all out in the world rising in the distance.

And yet winter has just begun.

■

Keith Parkes

What, exactly, does Keith Parkes have to do with Arch Stanton?

And why does the name Arch Stanton sound vaguely familiar?

Both very, very good questions.

During our absolutely fabulous two-week 2012 visit to Scotland, Jenn and I planned several pretty significant excursions. One of those was a tour of Orkney, which, like many tours in Scotland, is not something one accomplishes in an afternoon. It requires a ninety-minute ferry ride from Scrabster, on the very northern tip of Scotland, and you have to book passage on the ferry well in advance.

Because Scrabster was a good four-plus hours away from our base of operations near Nairn, and because the Orkney ferry sailed at 7:00 AM, we planned a two-day trip for this particular excursion.

Necessarily sight-unseen, the accommodation I booked for a single night was at a B&B near Thurso.

From the online booking page, it looked like it was near a working fisherman's port off a busy two-lane thoroughfare. I couldn't have been more wrong.

When we arrived at Thurso, the Dunnet Head B&B was nowhere to be found—and finding things in Thurso isn't all that complicated. A quick inquiry with another B&B operator clued us in that the location we sought was a fifteen-minute drive outside Thurso on the road to the Dunnet Head lighthouse.

Just about the time I was ready to turn back to Thurso because the road to Dunnet Head was becoming decidedly single-track and remote, and because not even a desolate cottage was in sight across the blasted heath, we espied Dunnet Head B&B.

Literally in the middle of nowhere.

And right next door, equally in the middle of nowhere, aside from its proximity to Dunnet Head B&B, stood Keith Parkes' "Rustic Interiors" Highland studio.

As Jenn and I were hauling our gear into the B&B I noticed in the golden-hour light that Keith's "Open" sign was out along the gravel shoulder of the road, and while Jenn settled in I strode next door to see what variety of artwork Mr. Parkes had to offer.

Before I saw a single item within the walls of his showroom, I encountered the most serendipitous and joy-inducing work of craftsmanship I have ever seen.

Propped against the drive's gatepost, *a propos* of nothing and yet of everything, was a replica of Arch Stanton's grave marker from Sergio Leone's *The Good, the Bad and the Ugly*. I simply stood there and laughed.

I have never, ever been so completely delighted by an unexpected treat.

I found my new and instantly bonded friend Keith sitting in front of a vintage cast-iron garden bench and giving it a fresh coat of green enamel. We talked easily and at length about our fondness for Leone's *outre* Italian-Spanish homages to the American West, and my private tour of the contents of his studio—reclaimed antiques, handcrafted wood-work, curios, and Keith's own photography—left me simply wonderstruck.

This was the art studio of my dreams—a gold mine for an interior designer. If I were independently wealthy and had a 10,000-square-foot home, I'd be Keith's patron saint.

One of the delights of social media sites is seeing things like Keith's from-the-springs-up recreation of a gypsy caravan pop up in your feed. Thanks to Facebook, I am regularly reminded of my magical encounter on the lonely road to Dunnet Head.

What a gift that was, and what a gift Keith's art continues to be.

Mindwalk

"It's a sign!"

I freely confess that I am prone to reading messages from the universe into the most commonplace of occurrences. It's the scientist in me.

> Probabilities are not probabilities of things, but probabilities of interconnections.

Many may read my writing and think, "Well, it figures that Greg would say such things, because Greg is an artist and a pastor. He doesn't have to make sense or be practical." And they write off my worldview as a symptom of wishful thinking. After all, the world is made of concrete facts, right? Not mere feelings about things.

> For physicists a particle has no independent existence. A particle is essentially a set of relations that reach outward to connect with other things.

Well, it was indeed the arts that taught me that I do have a unique talent for seeing the interconnectedness of things. And one of the connections that I made while I was studying at the University of Washington was the similarities between the sciences and the arts. Both are disciplined ways of making sense of the world and communicating something about that truth.

> The essential nature of matter lies not in objects, but in interconnections.

In the attempt to make sense of the world, it's natural to distill humanity into "two kinds of people," as Sergio Leone so eloquently pointed out in *The Good, the Bad and the Ugly*. Yet we are so reductionist and wrong when we do so. In reality, there is but one kind of person, and that one kind is infinite, and infinitely variable.

> Physicists are simply proving that what we call an object... an atom, a molecule, a particle... is only an approximation, a metaphor.

We may find it convenient to divide the world up into Liberal and Conservative, Republican and Democrat, reasonable and unreasonable, sane and insane, brilliant and stupid. But that's because the world is terribly inconvenient. Things are never as simple as dismissive labels.

> At the subatomic level, an object dissolves into a series of interconnections like chords of music. It's beautiful.

So while we may like the idea of boundaries and even find them practical and useful, they are in fact illusory. We can no more isolate ourselves from other things and other people— or other countries—than we can shun our hands or build a wall between our leg and our hip.

> That's a metaphor we can understand.

Were I to wall off my leg from my hip, both would continue to exist; but the ways in which they relate to each other would be dramatically changed.

> There is a continual exchange of matter and energy between my hand and this wood... between the wood and the air... and even between you and me.

So if it's true that everything is interconnected, what do we do with that information?

My choice is to actively work against the tendency toward reductionism—to reject easy and dismissive labels. To understand the real relationships between one thing and another rather than search for evidence that justifies my inertia toward isolationism.

As I move through life, I'm looking for ways in which the universe is trying to tell me, "This is connected to that. Everything is random, yet nothing is."

Ultimately, whether we like it or not, we're all part of one inseparable web of relationships. Even how I think about a stranger on the opposite side of the world—someone I have never even met or whom I am not even sure exists—has an impact on my perception of reality... perhaps even upon reality itself.

So I look for signs. Signs and wonders. And the very act of looking affects my experience of the world.

Sometimes the signs come from movies like 1990's *Mindwalk*, co-written by physicist Fritjof Capra: the film from which the quotes in this essay are taken. It's a two-hour conversation between a poet, a politician, and a physicist, and it delves deeply into the nuances and implications of Systems Theory as part of a vision for moving beyond the seeming mess in which we are currently mired.

But sometimes the signs come in the form of actual signs, too.

Like a couple days before Christmas when I was driving to Allyn, thinking about how wonderful life can be... and I passed a sign for Wright Bliss Road.

Talk about giving one pause.

I stopped to snap a photo, something I learned from Jenn.

> Even with the best intentions in the world you'll go wrong if you forget that life is infinitely more than yours or my obtuse theories about it. Healing the universe is an inside job, and you've helped me.
>
> And I love you. Every one of you.

■

Styx

You know what? I can be wonderstruck by Styx any time I want. I'm fifty-six years old, and I've earned the right.

There was a time I was downright embarrassed by my love of Styx. Queen I could justify on purely artistic grounds; The Moody Blues were "oldies" and didn't count. But during loud, pompous college dorm discussions about Elvis Costello, Bruce Springsteen, Rush, The Ramones, and Chrissie Hynde, Styx was decidedly unstylish.

"Mr. Roboto" did not help at all, of course; but some parts of myself I simply did not respect.

> We'll search for tomorrow
> On every shore
> And I'll try, oh, Lord I'll try
> To carry on

Grand Illusion was released in 1977, during my sophomore year in high school, and I was not alone in being taken away by it. At that time, I was just beginning to discover that life was not uniformly awful and that it was possible, to a degree, to be the captain of your own ship. Styx' nose-thumbing optimism appealed to me greatly.

I was ready to leave the bullying and the anger behind, to create the new me. An untouchable me. I would be above it all.

By my freshman year in college, I was well into that re-creation. But the new me was not happy. I was an academic success, but I was dead inside. I distinctly remember riding with my sister, Elane, in her metallic-red 1965 Impala SuperSport on the Viaduct. It was a dreary January afternoon in 1980, and we were on the way to the Coliseum to see Styx; and I felt... nothing.

> I think of childhood friends
> And the dreams we had
> We lived happily forever
> So the story goes
> But somehow we missed out
> On that pot of gold

I told Elane about that deadness... and something changed after that concert.

Now, after nearly forty years, I finally understand what changed. I understand because "Come Sail Away" popped up on the radio last night as I was driving home in the blowing snow after a screening of *An Appalachian Dawn*—a film about the revitalization of Clay County, Kentucky. It's a story about broken dreams and no rainbows, much less pots of gold... but also about carrying on, about the search for tomorrow.

And about getting there.

> A gathering of angels
> Appeared above my head
> They sang to me this song of hope
> And this is what they said
> They said, Come sail away

Come—sail away; it's not enough to simply carry on. There's more to life than that.

That's what changed on the night of January 17, 1980. I started to live with hope.

It's something we all need.

■

Emmanuel

While packing up the last of my Christmas decorations, I am listening to random selections from my music collection.

Just as I am about to carry an armload of boxes down to the basement, an arresting melody cuffs me to the doorknob.

> My vision's clouded by a thousand doubts tonight
> The air I breathe feels heavy in my lungs
> My heart is shrouded by a cool dull ache inside
> As I cast a vacant stare up to the sky
> I'm looking for an answer, I want more than just all right
> I want more than half a feeling I'll make it through the night
> More than just a shadow; I want breathing flesh and bone
> So I'm trusting in your promise that I don't have to be alone

The words, so poignant. The voice, so haunting, so beautiful.

> Would you take my sunken eyes and help me see?
> Fill me with a power greater than the air I breathe?
> I want to speak your name until the weight is lifted.
> Would you sing to me an easy melody?
> Oh, such an easy melody.

As I stand there, I think, *This is the most beautiful thing I've ever heard.* And then she sings:

> Emmanuel, Emmanuel
> We want a hope that's greater than the storybooks can tell
> Emmanuel, Emmanuel
> It's the sound of freedom breaking in; God with us to dwell

This is a Christmas song, too! Oh my gosh! Why can't I place it? I listen to my Christmas music collection constantly through November and December!

I know that voice! Is it Battistelli? Is it Ginny Owens? One of the Barlow girls?

I unshackle myself from my burdensome load and cross the room. I pick up my MP3 player and on the screen it tells me: Jenny Snipstead.

Of course.

Jenny is a friend.

Several years ago, I collected miscellaneous singles that she had recorded both solo and as part of the Soma Music collective in Tacoma. I listen to *The Story* (Volumes I and II) regularly, and it was through those albums that my late wife, Jenn, and I came to know Jenny and her music. Jenn was particularly moved by "Watchman," a song that loomed large for Jenn as she drew closer and closer to the end of her life.

Jenny Snipstead is now Jenny Jones, married and living in L.A. pursuing her music career as Willow Stephens. I did not recognize her voice on this song simply because it has remained hidden in my 4000-track music collection as uncategorized miscellany.

How ironic, given the lyric that follows:

> Night is falling on blank pages and blank walls
> It buries every single song I write
> And the rain keeps falling, pouring down on every side
> The numbing rhythm leaves me paralyzed

This is a song for life in transition, for times when we are on our way from one place to another, feeling rooted in neither, wondering if we will ever feel like we belong.

> My hope is in a question, in a man I've yet to see
> And I find in songs unwritten, that I find a sweet release
> It's not how I imagined, not some simple, happy end
> But it's one who knows the ache I feel: a savior and a friend

"Emmanuel" is at its sweetest as it settles quietly and gently into its final stanza:

> He takes my sunken eyes to help me see
> He fills me with a power greater than the air I breathe
> When I speak his name I feel the weight is lifted
> He fills me with an easy melody

Whatever success an artist achieves in life, nothing can be more meaningful than this: to create work which fuels people through their loneliest days, inspiring them to reach for "hope that's even greater than the storybooks can tell." Willow has been making that happen for years, though she may not be aware—or may not even believe it to be true if she is aware.

This is a common doubt with artists. As I Google the track, I am wonderstruck now by the lyric's listing on Bandcamp. Above the opening stanza is a single word that is not actually sung:

Hope

Tears come to my eyes.

This is what I need to end my week. "It's the sound of freedom breaking in."

∎

Bill Murray

I finally got around to watching *The Bill Murray Stories: Life Lessons Learned from a Mythical Man*. So fitting that I should wrap my month up that way, as saturated as January has been in hope.

The film—which, as a film, as not nearly as compelling as its subject—documents the ways in which Murray has become legendary for simply dropping into the lives of everyday people. He has no agent, entourage, or PR people telling him what to do or not do, so he turns up in very unexpected places.

A bloke named Tom Wright, for example, is a Scot who was at a house party on Hope Street near St. Andrews. "All of a sudden, there's a bit of a noise in the next room," recalls Wright in the film, "so I wandered through to the kitchen, and lo and behold, I'm standing there with my beer in my hand looking across the kitchen… and Bill Murray is talking to a few girls."

Murray then told the girls to get back to the party while he'd take care of the dishes. Which he did, washing, rinsing, and drying plates and glasses.

"He hung around for a while" after that, continues Wright, "had a couple of drinks, and then made his way into the night."

And Wright's impression of the incident? "The stories that involve him are Bill interacting in an everyday manner, and it removes that barrier, that Chinese wall, between the rest of us and celebrity—and I think that's the effect he has on people. If that means you go away feeling good about yourself, then that's quite a nice thing."

Gavin Edwards, who has analyzed the phenomenon extensively, goes a little further: "I think Bill Murray teaches us a few things. One is not to live life on autopilot." Tommy Avallone, the documentary's director, says that Murray "comes into people's lives, gets a feel for the room, and then makes the moment something special."

Since it's Avallone's film, he gets the final word in tracing the roots of Murray's passion for "being in the moment." And it does appear to be in Murray's roots with the Second City improv group in Chicago, studying under Del Close. Those with experience in the troupe say that Close counseled Murray and other legendary Second City vets "not to fear anything." The idea was to be open to everything, "saying yes to the other person's idea" and "go with it." It produces infinite possibilities.

The effect of the "Yes—and…" approach to life can be intoxicating. As Susan Messing says in the film, you can tell when people are living this way because, as with Bill Murray's everyday life, they are "simply reveling in where they are. Improv might be the only time in my life where I get to slow down and enjoy exactly where I am."

Pop psychology calls this "being present and available." Edie Dillon lauds it as "serendipity." Mary Oliver says, "listening."

Consider this story directly from Bill Murray's lips, about his ride with a cab driver "who's a saxophone player."

> I said, "When do you practice it?"
>
> "I don't know... I drive like fourteen hours a day or something like that."
>
> "Where's your sax?"
>
> "It's in the trunk."
>
> "Look, you know that's two and two: it makes four. Pull over and get in the trunk. I know how to drive a car."
>
> Not only did he play all the way to Sausalito, which is a long ways, we stopped and got barbecue... What people would call a sketchy rib place in Oakland at like 2:15 in the morning...
>
> It made for a beautiful night.

And Murray ends his story with the remark that he finds such incidents perfectly natural—that he's merely doing what anyone would do under the same circumstances.

Well, yes—if you believe that everything matters. And especially that *people* matter.

To be fair, I doubt that you or I—or Ice Cube or Alexandria Ocasio-Cortez—would be as welcome dropping into random strangers' lives. Murray enjoys a unique level of privilege.

Nonetheless, I dare say that we could all benefit from slowing down and reveling in where we are, at all times.

No matter where we might be.

I've certainly been reveling in life lately and enjoying where I am... and hope for more of the same!

■

Springsteen

I never imagined I'd be writing about metaphysics in response to a Bruce Springsteen concert, but there ya go. Some things simply can't be explained.

> Metaphysics is the branch of philosophy that examines the fundamental nature of reality…

Bruce Springsteen on Broadway, featuring material from his one-man-plus show, recently surfaced on Netflix. I sat down to watch it last night and was not surprised to find it chock-full of creative storytelling. And quotable material, which I have included in this essay.

I was surprised, however, to find Bruce copping to much sleight-of-artistic-hand with his music, chalking most of his success up to "magic." After all, he says, he had precious little experience with most of the things about which he sang. "I'm that good," he comments semi-sarcastically.

Art isn't magic, though. As much as "write what you know" is taught to aspiring authors, it turns out that there are a great many aspects of the human experience about which we become experts without living them first-hand.

Artists just tend to be very observant. And because of that they see a lot of potential in the world.

> …including the relationship between mind and matter…

My favorite bit on this front was The Boss talking about The E Street Band, and the intangibles that made it great. As many people have observed, it is generally true that the sum of the parts is often greater than the whole. And as great as Springsteen and Clarence Clemons, in particular, were individually, something truly magical happened when they came together with Little Steven, Danny Federici, Garry Tallent, Roy Bittan, and Max Weinberg.

"There is a communion of souls," Springsteen explains. "You're in search of something, an adventurous undertaking." And when you do that, he insists, "principles of math get stood on their head, and 1 + 1 = 3."

> Now, 1 + 1 = 2, that happens every day.
>
> And that's not magic. That's the grind. ... But when 1 + 1 = 3, that's when your life changes.
>
> You see everything new, and these are days when you are visited by visions. When the world around you brings down the Spirit, and you feel blessed to be alive."

Oh, how I have felt 1 + 1 = 3 this last year, when things shouldn't have added up at all. Particularly when a particular One was subtracted from my life. But Springsteen understands the mathematics of the Divine, the dynamics of the universe. How intangibles cannot be accounted for by equations. Because 1 + 1 = 3, he says, "is the essential equation of love."

I like that.

I *love* that.

"It is," he says, "the reason the Universe will never be fully comprehensible."

> ...between substance and attribute, and between possibility and actuality.

Do we *really* want to be able to understand the universe? I think not. What kind of universe would an understandable one be?

An existence of pure actuality, devoid of possibility.

All 1 + 1 = 2. No surprises.

Gah.

■

Temptation

I was a pretty rebellious cuss thirty years ago.

Perhaps I still am. All I know is that major life change seems to happen every ten years for me: relocation to Twisp in 2018, adjustment to life with Jenn's disability in 2008, the Road Taken in 1998…

And this story, from 1988, also a major point of departure.

Have you ever heard a movie trailer intone, *Her life would never be the same again…*? If you have heard it once, I imagine you've heard variations hundreds of times. Transformative experiences are a staple of the cinematic marketing machine.

But most of what Hollywood has to offer us is so clichéd as to render the concept toothless. After all, our lives are always mutable, and we are never the same as we once were. It's not possible to remain the same. As motivational speakers will tell you, you are either getting better or you are getting worse; the question is, then, what *are* we becoming?

What the trailers are really trying to tell us, of course, is that their characters are experiencing some truly remarkable change. Well, Martin Scorsese's *The Last Temptation of Christ* produced that kind of remarkable change in me, and my life certainly did chart a new course after that screening.

In 1988 I was drifting along in my engineering career. In August, I had just completed producing and directing my short film *Who Shall Stand* and was feeling pretty bored with software. Compared to producing films, the challenges were looking awfully small.

Spiritually, I was awake, but on another level I was also kind of sleepwalking.

One Sunday morning, preacher Roy Stedman told our church congregation that we should avoid seeing *The Last Temptation of Christ*. It showed Jesus having sex with Mary Magdalene and claimed that he came down off the cross and lived and died as an ordinary man. It was blasphemous and would destroy a person's faith.

I was not particularly a fan of Scorsese's films and hadn't really planned on seeing *Temptation*; but being twenty-six, Greg, and generally consumed by cinema—thus quite knowledgeable about the film just via film journals, and certainly far more knowledgeable than a fine preacher whose primary domain was the Bible and not Scorsese—I couldn't resist the intellectual and artistic challenge. Or the chance to ignore pastoral advice.

So on Wednesday that week, I skipped out of work early and wandered over to the Cinerama to catch a matinee.

The opening of the film is arresting. Even those who hate *Temptation* agree that Peter Gabriel's score is one of the all-time greats, evoking a palpably tonal Semitic apocalypse. An adult Jesus on the verge of beginning his ministry is literally tortured by the Spirit descending on him not like a dove but like a raptor, and he sees himself more as dithering lunatic than burgeoning messiah. Willem Dafoe is the perfect Jesus.

The film has its faults, of course, and they become quickly apparent. Its primary fault is its budget, which dictates a guerrilla film style with characterizations, performances, and accents that feel more workshopped than very well-thought-through. But I would argue at length with anyone who says the script is poor.

Key to understanding and appreciating the film (which I don't expect anyone to rush out to do) is the question of the film's and book's titular temptation.

The "supposition," to co-opt a critical dialectic from C.S. Lewis, is that the greatest temptation Jesus faced was to simply be an ordinary man rather than the Christ. In Kazantzakis' supposition, the moment when Jesus is most vulnerable to that temptation is when he is hanging on the cross—and Satan comes to him in the guise of an adolescent angel, presenting him with a detailed vision of what that future could look like for him, if he would just renounce God's will and leave the cross behind.

And so, for forty-odd minutes, Scorsese leads us with Jesus on a fast-forward tour through this living vision—coupling and cohabitating with Mary Magdalene, grieving her premature death, siring children with Lazarus' sisters Mary and Martha, encountering a creepily convicted and conspiratorial Apostle Paul (very effectively portrayed by the late Harry Dean Stanton). Eventually we find this alter-Jesus lying on his deathbed awaiting the consequences of natural causes.

But Judas creeps into the vision, spoiling the illusion that Satan has so cleverly crafted, and the aged Jesus crawls his way back out of the ghastly dream and onto the cross to claim his rightful place as God's obedient son.

I found a good many scenes in the film remarkable—Jesus' fasting in the wilderness, Andre Gregory's John the Baptist, Jesus' first on-screen encounter with Magdalene, Stanton's portrayal of Saul/Paul. But what really struck me, and profoundly so, was the presentation and conception of that central temptation. The film's and book's contrived relationship between Jesus and Mary is of course absurd, even childish; but the idea that living an ordinary life can be a powerful temptation is pretty profound. After all, isn't that the American dream?

That's what I saw Scorsese portray onscreen, in a particularly first-century Judean fashion. In 1988 I didn't have the theological sophistication or scriptural knowledge to observe that God is able to do far more than we ask or imagine, but my heart told me something more concrete: God wants a lot more for us than a two-car garage, 1.4 kids, and a white picket fence. One helluva lot more.

And as I sat through the film's closing credits, I said to myself, "You know, in particular, God wants one helluva lot more from me than this nine-to-five grind, nachos and margaritas on demand, and Seahawk season tickets. I've been running from God all my life, living the temptation rather than the calling. And I didn't even have to come down off a cross to do it. I really have no idea what God wants from me, but I guarantee it's not what I'm doing now.

"It's time for a change."

What I didn't realize at the time, and this is pretty profound, is that God had already prepared that change for me. As I walked out into the hazy afternoon light behind the Cinerama after the screening, I clutched in my hand a copy of a movie news rag that was published by one of the Seattle area film exhibitors. I had read through it before the screening of *Temptation* began and had run across an advertisement for Redwood Theater's auditions for *The Hound of the Baskervilles*.

The ad had intrigued me because of my experience directing *Who Shall Stand*. "If I'm going to continue directing actors," thought I, "I'd best get to know some better actors—not to mention get some real acting experience myself."

And so, seemingly unrelated to my spiritual and emotional awakening that day, I left that screening of *The Last Temptation of Christ* with that movie news rag rolled up in my right hand and Redwood Theater's phone number circled. The rest, as they say, is history—but a story for another day.

"What are we becoming?"

Indeed. I dare say we have precious little idea. But the universe is hard at work on us nonetheless.

■

1812

The things the universe wants to give back to us.

This afternoon during my lunch break I was watching "The Rehearsal," Season 1 Episode 5 of *Mozart in the Jungle*. A Confluence Gallery colleague recently became the second person to recommend the 2014 show to me, so I started picking my way through thirty-minute installments yesterday.

In "The Rehearsal," a temperamental and impetuous conductor takes his orchestra on a field trip. In lieu of their usual controlled environs, they climb through a gap in a chain-link fence to set up shop in a vacant Manhattan lot. And instead of the regularly scheduled program…

Well, let's just say I was wildly surprised and in awe of what came next.

Rodrigo calls his musicians to play from memory a very familiar piece: Tchaikovsky's *1812 Overture*. And from my own memory, the opening strains of the London Symphony Orchestra's recording of the seminal opus came to my ears.

I also weep now just to think of it.

Tchaikovsky is not my favorite composer; that would be Dvořák. But Russian composers, with their flair for theatrics and musical melodrama, do touch my soul—and *1812* is my favorite from that front.

In college, "classical" music was one of my staples. Before I headed to class for exams, and finals in particular, I would don headphones, recline on my dorm bed, and indulge in twelve to twenty minutes of sonic peace. On one occasion, Tchaikovsky's *Marche Slave* literally took me to an out-of-body experience. I aced the final.

But *1812*... I had—and still have; I'm looking at it right now—a Deutsche Grammophon pressing of Fiedler conducting the Boston Pops, with a battery of 12-gauge shotguns standing in for the cannon. But it's not the brass and bells and percussion that grab me. It's the strings, the lyrical patience and passion with which they build to those powerful peals and explosions.

Oh, how I have missed those strains. Where have they gone, over the years? I cannot say. But this afternoon they unexpectedly came rushing back.

The brilliance of Roman Coppola's direction in this episode overwhelmed me, capturing the magic of art and music and their power to bring a community together.

Should you watch *Mozart in the Jungle*? I have no idea. Should you screen "The Rehearsal"? Got me. I doubt you'd find there exactly what I did.

But... The universe wants to return things to us... a lost earring, perhaps, or an overture to living.

What next? I can't wait.

■

Dissonance

On Saturday night, December 7, 2002, Jenn and I were on stage together for the closing scene of *Homecoming*, the final entry of the Chi-Rho Files plays developed by the Dramatic Insights Ministries theatrical collective.

The series was an alternate-present drama that essentially retold the story of the 1st century Christian Church in the context of a fictional late-20th-century fascist-imperialist North American vassal state.

> I have lived with a fragile faith, built on the ether of vague memories, and hunches that I could neither prove nor explain. Why?
>
> When I was twelve, my sister was taken from me: taken from our home by a will that I came to believe was supernatural. This belief sustained me, fueling a quest for truths that were as elusive as my memories. It even brought me home, finally, to now find life in the midst of death.
>
> They took the resistance fighters first, executed them one by one. A short time ago they took the first of the Christians. Before long it should all be over.

Those lines, adapted in homage to the *X-Files* Season 2 episode "Colony," were read by Jenn in voiceover while Ana and Nico, the characters Jenn and I played, awaited execution.

> What has happened here in Philadelphia has justified every belief. If I should die now, it will be with a certainty that my faith has been righteous.
>
> And if through death larger mysteries are revealed, I will have already learned the answer to the question that has driven me here: that there is a will in the universe greater than our own; that it was made flesh, and walked among us; that there are indeed true believers among us, and that nothing—neither death, nor life, nor angels, nor principalities, nor things present, nor things to come, nor powers, nor height, nor depth, nor any other created thing—can prevail against them.

These were words Jenn came to believe very, very strongly over the next fifteen years.

At the time we played our roles in *Homecoming*, we really had no clue about the long, slow road to death that she was about to begin walking, or the great irony of the scene we were playing—or the true significance of the title I had chosen for the play.

Homecoming was a drama about cognitive dissonance, about the ways in which the things we seek, and the ways in which we go about seeking them, often become obstacles to the finding. For the play's pre-show, intermission, and curtain-call music, I selected tracks from Ennio Morricone's soundtrack to the Russian-Italian film *The Red Tent*, which starred Sean Connery and Peter Finch—the story of an ill-fated dirigible expedition to the North Pole.

The music, some themes of which Morricone would later recycle for *The Untouchables*, is itself full-on 1960s avant-garde dissonance. At times, it incorporates various non-instrumental sounds: human voices, metallic screeches, radioed Morse code distress calls.

Initially, Jenn was very put off by the use of that music for the production; but as rehearsals progressed, she saw that the dissonance of the music harmonized with the dissonance of our characters' lives in a unique and powerful way.

I was listening to the *Red Tent* soundtrack again for the first time in many years during my drive from Des Moines back to Twisp the other day. As I passed through snowy landscapes that would not have been out of place in that film, I thought again about incongruity and the role that it plays in shaping our lives.

Those who like to talk most about cognitive dissonance seem to think that they themselves are free from it. What could be more ironic or cognitively dissonant? None of us lives an intellectually consistent life.

But if we yearn to live so, where would we be without dissonance? Those jarring notes are the only clues we have to the path toward positive change. Discord plays the tune which stands out amidst the crowd of otherwise ear-tickling self-justifications. Bread crumbs to mark the path home.

Jenn lived a life in search of dissonance, knowing that the quest was not to avoid it as the chart of life progressed—but to place her hands on the piano's keys in such a way that they remained true to the closing chords while they resolved as written: to simply be at peace with the notes, much in the same way that *Homecoming* closed, or that Grace saturated her own final months in the midst of titanic pain and hardship.

Music. What a beautiful metaphor for life!

Let's go home.

∎

The Fault in Our Stars

I very, very rarely click my TV's remote control "just to see what's on." Why? Because 99% of the time I know that the answer will be "nothing."

Sunday night was an exception.

About 10:00 PM, a little late for idle entertainment, I flooded my living room with soft blue light and saw that FXM was showing *The Fault in Our Stars*. The only thing I knew about it was that it was vaguely in the back of my head as a short-list candidate for screening after I saw an interview with Willem Dafoe in which the project was mentioned.

I came in about two minutes late, having missed only the narrative which introduces the film: "I believe we have a choice in this world," says Hazel, "about how to tell sad stories."

> On the one hand, you can sugarcoat it, the way they do in movies and romance novels where beautiful people learn beautiful lessons and nothing is too messed up that can't be fixed with an apology and a Peter Gabriel song. I like that way as much as the next girl, believe me. It's just not the truth. *This* is the truth. Sorry.

Thence follows a story about a couple of beautiful young (gravely ill) people who learn beautiful (if very painful and even fatal) lessons to the tune of Ed Sheeran and the like.

Yet instead of the self-conscious bait-and-switch, it does tell a lot of truth about being gravely ill and about living through that illness until the living comes to an end. And I found the opening scene in a support group for terminal teens instantly arresting.

I didn't finish the movie Sunday night but did add it to "My Stuff" in Hulu to DVR for followup on Monday. Though the film has its own share of Fairy-Tale window-dressing—and hey, why wouldn't it, given that it takes several million dollars to get a movie like this made?—it drives quotably toward a literate, very poignant, and convincingly moving conclusion.

"You don't get to choose if you get hurt in this world," writes one of the characters. "But you do have a say in who hurts you.

"And I like my choices."

Yeah, that's a truth that I have lived.

And I remain wonderstruck.

■

Hollywood Jesus

Thanks to a dream about "The Master of Disaster" the other night, I was reminded that I was part of something pretty darned special for nearly 15 years.

"MOD" was a nickname for writer Maurice Broaddus, one of the earliest of the long-time contributors to web-publishing phenomenon *Hollywood Jesus*—the "pop culture from a spiritual point of view" brainchild of pastor and media specialist David Bruce.

> Hollywood Jesus is way out past Pluto somewhere, where there are bodies trying to resist the gravitational pull of the Church and launch themselves into the nether regions of the Milky Way.

The point is: I had a dream about Maurice on Tuesday night. In the dream, I showed up late to a fete celebrating the life work of Mr. Broaddus. That was a little odd, considering that he's still quite alive and kicking, and that he's not exactly ready to head out to pasture. (I might also observe that he's a good deal younger than me, but that's not saying much, given my own senior citizen status.)

Anyway... I show up late and miss most of the career tributes broadcast to the gathering by the emcee, who was conducting short interviews with Maurice's past colleagues. As a result, there wasn't much of a queue waiting to speak, and I didn't need much patience to wait my turn. Soon I was seated in front of a microphone.

> Given that there are so many other sites telling you whether a movie is safe for your family or morally repugnant, or how many breasts are exposed, or how many swear words there are, we instead ask what positives can be found.

"When I first started editing Maurice's work at *Hollywood Jesus*," I began, "I had not been there long, coming on board in 1999 as David Bruce's personal editor. Maurice was one of the early fixtures on the site, along with Darrel Manson and Mike Furches, and he specialized in coverage of horror films—and other things that 'churchy' people don't much care for..."

I trailed off because I could see the emcee's eyes start to glaze over. He was bored out of his mind, stood up, and just wandered off. I've had a lot of media experience, but that was pretty unique.

> What are you going to do? Start complaining because people are broken and sinful? We know that. We're all broken. You can't whine about that.

I went in search of Maurice, who was off having a private little soiree-within-a-party. When I tracked him down, he smiled broadly and toothy, as only Broaddus can, and I began to tell him what had just happened... and he, too, became quickly bored and drifted away to find a more interesting conversation!

I woke thinking that I had just been the worst possible kind of party crasher. Ugh.

When I sat down for my morning Facebook crawl, a post on Maurice's timeline popped up in my feed, with an amusing tidbit about an upcoming photo shoot for a magazine cover. "Huh," I thought. Not so unlike Maurice, who hosts MoCon (yes, his own writers' convention) annually. And not so unlike my dream.

I really *am* chopped liver. Ho, hum.

> If we devote six to twelve years of education as children to learning a language we already speak, English, then why should we not invest time in learning the language of film?

So I chimed in with the general celebratory mood of the thread and mentioned my fresh dream about the MoBro. Other writers from the HJ stable, such as Mr. Furches, Mark Allen Sommer, and Mark Ezra Stokes chimed in. Naturally. Cuz when Maurice posts something, usually two or three hundred people jump on it.

> And the uninitiated's reaction to the idea of "Hollywood Jesus: Pop Culture from a Spiritual Point of View" was yesterday what it was twenty years ago: "Wow. That sounds interesting. I'd read that!"

Yes. Literally millions of people did. There is no high wall that separates Christians from culture. We are the culture, we are in the culture, and the culture influences us.

HJ was already a viral phenomenon by the time *The Lord of the Rings* and *The Passion of the Christ* came around; but our coverage of those projects pushed site traffic into the stratosphere. At its peak, the site was publishing roughly a dozen movie reviews a week—covering just about every new theatrical release—plus coverage of TV, music, books, and games. I coordinated a staff of twenty-plus volunteer contributors, and Jenn and I edited it all… some three million words or so each year. We published annual collections of movie reviews in paperback. God, it was fun.

> We are, essentially, all on the same side. Or rather, we are all the ground over which spiritual battles are fought. That should bring us together, not cast us over against one another.

As I was prepping this essay, I came across a lengthy 2010 interview I did with Timothy Dalrymple for *Patheos*, detailing the history of the website. The quotes scattered through this essay are taken from that interview. Apparently I did not bore *him* to death!

> Film is visceral. It satisfies deep emotional and spiritual cravings in a fashion that is so efficient and powerful that we can't get enough of it. It is the crack cocaine of the art world. It's less a religious than an addictive experience.

In a footnote of great irony, the demise of *Hollywood Jesus* went largely unnoticed.

Yesterday I stopped by the site, which underwent a major overhaul in 2012 after I left. Only our Last Man Standing, former Games editor Johann Snyder, continues to post content to the site. The site's final paid editor appears to have made the last "ranking" article one year ago.

Yo is a good man, and his faithfulness to the cause is remarkable, given the site's commercial mismanagement. Or rather, the inevitable commercialization of a ministry.

The bulk of the writers jumped ship in 2013 to join my editorial successor's site, *ScreenFish*. Jacob Sahms and his team of veterans there, including Mark Allen Sommer and Darrel Manson, have done a sweet job carrying on with David Bruce's vision.

> Film, like all art, is a form of communication. It doesn't require offense. It doesn't require any more of a perception of threat than you have in a conversation with your neighbor.

∎

George Harrison

Somehow, by the time I was ten years old, I was diligently following George Harrison's development as an artist… and, I suspect, as a man.

How did I manage this? I have no idea. I suppose I was just as media-aware as any child born in 1962—"it happened at the World's Fair," after all—but still: From where was I getting my information? TV? My sister's *Tiger Beat* magazines?

Could have been the radio, I suppose, since I started listening to my dad's wonky transistor radio at night in fifth grade because I couldn't get to sleep.

> I look at you all, see the love there that's sleeping
> While my guitar gently weeps
> I look at the floor and I see it needs sweeping
> Still my guitar gently weeps

But The Beatles were not a staple in our household.

The first single I bought was Paul Revere and the Raiders' "Indian Reservation," and that wasn't until 1971… fully a year after The Beatles had broken up. And when that news broke, while the family was driving on I-5 into downtown Seattle, I distinctly remember thinking, "Who are The Beatles?"

How, then, you may well ask, can I be sure I was diligently following George Harrison, given my ignorance of music in general and The Beatles in particular?

Because over the last couple of days I watched the 3.5-hour documentary *George Harrison: Living in the Material World* on Netflix, and discovered that I had, in fact, fully digested much of this information as a child... and retained it all.

Why else would Klaus Voorman, Jim Keltner, and Billy Preston seem so familiar to me?

In particular, I had tracked the fact that the songs Harrison had written with The Beatles ("Something" and "While My Guitar Gently Weeps," in particular) were of a distinctly different flavor than those of his bandmates; that he seemed to set out recording songs with a very purposeful bent following the breakup of the band; that the subject matter of his music was different than most of the stuff on the radio, with a decidedly spiritual bent (which was obvious, of course); that his 1971 Concert for Bangladesh was a truly groundbreaking and selfless event; and that he himself was one serious dude.

I think his seriousness appealed terribly to me, given that I was such a serious kid as well.

The details I gleaned of his spiritual quest deeply impressed me, too. I apparently correctly discerned that his concern was not "getting it right," as seemed to be the case with most of the churchy people in my young world; instead it was growth, plain and simple. And a deep desire that others should grow, too.

And not the desire that others should join the ranks of the "woke," or other such trendy contemporary labels which imply that there are distinctions to be made between "the sleeping" and "the wakeful," the latter of whom get to lecture their lessers while patting themselves on the back; no. Just the simple recognition that we are all asleep, to one degree or another, and that there is a great deal of wakefulness left for us all to discover.

> What I know, I can do
> If I give my love now to everyone like you
> But if it's not love that you need
> Then I'll try my best to make everything succeed

Here comes the sun. My sweet Lord!

> Please take hold of my hand, that I might understand you

■

C.S. Lewis

I must confess my chagrin at having to type the title of this note… but I suppose it was a foregone conclusion that I could not avoid writing about Clive Staples Lewis forever.

I became sick of writing about Lewis by the end of 2008, and my public career as an "internationally known lecturer on film, J.R.R. Tolkien, and C.S. Lewis" wound down with a bombshell lecture at Baylor in January 2009. The title of my talk was "Inklings: Too Good for Hollywood, or Perfect Fit?"—and as the title of the lecture might suggest, my burned-out cynicism came down on the side of "Perfect Fit."

The talk was received with mostly stunned silence as I concluded with something on the order of, "Loud-mouthed grousing fans had best just get over the fact that Lewis and Tolkien sold the film rights to their books. They didn't *have* to. But they *did*. So if you have complaints to lodge, lodge them with the long-gone Inklings themselves, and not the studios or filmmakers."

I guess I thought that ten years as an expert in the field were enough.

My 1999 *Hollywood Jesus* essay on Tolkien's "legendarium" had gone viral at the turn of the century (back when "going viral" was something relatively new) and had been translated, without my knowing it, into Swedish and Spanish.

By 2004 I was Writer in Residence at Puget Sound Christian College; a published author of two books on Tolkien and Peter Jackson; sitting in on influential roundtable interviews with Peter Jackson, Philippa Boyens, and Fran Walsh; a regular on the *Lord of the Rings* convention circuit; lecturing at universities such as Aston, Belmont, and Notre Dame; and regularly annoying the hell out of Douglas Gresham (C.S. Lewis' stepson and "guardian" of the Lewis literary legacy; ha!).

This phase of notoriety culminated when Lewis expert Bruce Edwards declared my Past Watchful Dragons conference paper "Sometimes a Film May Say Best What's to Be Said" the highlight of the conference—and invited Jenn and I to author the closing chapter of the definitive four-volume *C.S. Lewis: Life, Works, and Legacy.*

That decade of relative celebrity was certainly flattering—and a tremendous distraction for Jenn in the midst of her physical decline. But the "need" to be an expert on Lewis became exceedingly tiresome. I could have gone on indefinitely had the subject matter been limited to Tolkien, probably, because his *oeuvre* was more or less confined (if one can call the multi-volume *History of Middle-earth* "confined").

But with Lewis… the literature was simply endless—and scattershot. The man was all over the map, with opinions about everything under the sun.

So after the dispiriting Oscars coverage with Jeffrey Overstreet and Jennie Spohr on Dick Staub's *Kindlings Muse* live podcast in 2009, I just walked away from the talking-head circuit, and newspapers eventually stopped calling me for comment.

I concluded my time as *Hollywood Jesus* Managing Editor four years later. Since then, I have studiously avoided reading more Lewis… but he has now managed to sneak in through my back door via an autobiographical book I picked up at Value Village, in which he features as a minor character.

But danged if the book doesn't include some Lewis letters not published elsewhere!

And ultra-danged if some of his words don't eerily echo something I wrote in 2012, just about the time that Jenn and I were leaving Lewis and Tolkien behind in favor of more ancient spiritual inspiration.

I wrote the following in response to a visualization exercise at a CFDM Northwest spiritual formation retreat on Hood Canal in September 2012—the first poem I had written in a very long time, and the beginning of my renewed interest in the poetic form. It's titled, "In the Dark."

> Only on stage is moonlight blue
> Silver also just poetic fancy
> In the woods at night
> All is many shades of darkness

Light may catch the crowns of trees
Or tops of scrub along the trail
But shadows fall most deeply
Where the outlines of fir
And vine maple
And fallen log
Or a stump
And salal
Converge
Darkly

Always in the lowest place
The spot you most want to see
Where your next footfall lies
The line your path must take

But darkness is the hardest thing to see
So to stay on the trail you look aside
Find your way in the periphery

There is no roadmap
There is no guide
There is no lamp
No shining beacon to bring you home
Just you and the path

And the next six steps

I was wonderstruck, then, after long years of shutting my mind to Lewis, his ideas, and his writing, to read the following words in a letter he wrote to Sheldon Vanauken regarding spiritual awakening:

A glimpse is not a vision. But to a man on a mountain road by night, a glimpse of the next three feet of road may matter more than a vision of the horizon.

Whoa.

At the time I wrote "In the Dark," I felt it to be almost heretical and was red in the face as I embarrassedly read it to my fellows. Aren't we, after all, supposed to find shining inspiration in faith?

But this is reality, that often the inspiration we find is what lies at our very feet.

Or unexpectedly, in the pages of a second-hand book on the first day of a new chapter in life.

Thanks, Jack, you old dog.

∎

Roger Taylor

1986, Seattle, Washington.

I'm sharing a house off Latona near Green Lake with John Adami. I'm pretty drunk on 750ml of a potent California cider, and I'm listening to Roger Taylor's 1984 solo album, *Strange Frontier*, for probably the 80th time.

Taylor's vibe has always gotten to me, from the first time I heard "I'm In Love With My Car" off Queen's *A Night at the Opera* in 1975. His lyrics are spare and usually pretty poppy, but they have always carried a sensitivity to the moral dilemma of ordinary people. At the moment, though, his cover of Bob Dylan's "Masters of War" is boring into my brain like an ethics hand grenade.

■

I don't think I was very aware of being young in 1986, even though I was just twenty-four.

> It's the sad-eyed, goodbye, yesterday moments I remember,
> It's the bleak street, weak-kneed partings I recall.

I was two years into my stint at Boeing Military Aircraft Company and seven years into my experiments with living "my way." I'd long ago ditched the "vertical hold" that Taylor wrote about in 1976's "Drowse," quoted throughout this essay, but the experiment had simply devolved into a lot of drinking and material excess. I was what they today call "a hot mess"—no everyday hero, but a whole bunch of zero. I wanted more reason for living or dying than the next case of cider and Friday Night Mixed Grill at The Unicorn on the Ave.

For whatever reason, Roger Taylor was the germ of my real quest for truth and a life of authenticity… though I couldn't have put that name to it then. I just knew that as I watched the slopes of Mt. Rainier pinken through the house's south-facing picture window, I was a purposeless fraud headed nowhere. I had to make changes, and I had to make big ones.

> Never wanted to be the boy next door,
> Always thought I'd be something more,
> But it ain't easy for a small town boy.

Change did come, quickly and radically. But that's another story.

This one is about Roger Taylor.

When much later Jenn and I got together and we started sharing our favorite music with each other, I of course filled her in on all things Queen, Elvis Costello, and Ennio Morricone. But there was also a special tour through Roger Taylor, too, including tracks both from Queen's albums and Taylor's solo LPs.

These days, it's cool that the film *Bohemian Rhapsody* is finally highlighting Taylor's remarkable vocal range—wider and higher than Freddie Mercury's—and the pivotal role that his persona and percussion played in Queen's success. These were some of the things I communicated to Jenn in 1998.

The session was prefaced with my usual Taylor disclaimer: "His lyrics are spare and not terribly serious, but he has a way with layering instrumentation, percussion, and vocalization that's very unique." I knew she'd get that, as an Enya fan. But she also very quickly picked up on the sneaky subtlety of Taylor's songwriting: Yes, he doesn't go for verbal gymnastics in his lyrics; but he knows that music can do a lot of the heavy lifting that poets have to accomplish solely via words. And he's content with that.

I distinctly remember Jenn's reaction to "Drowse," which I listened to on my drive back to Twisp this morning. "And you say he's not particularly poetic," she scoffed. "Ha!"

> Thinkin' it right, doin' it wrong
> It's easier from an arm chair,
> Waves of alternatives wash at my sleepiness,
> Have my eggs poached for breakfast I guess.

Jenn was right. For forty-plus years now, I have waxed philosophical over my breakfast eggs.

Thanks, Roger.

∎

Lee and Bianca

> Don't come around
> You have been warned
> You have been foolin' 'round on me
> Everybody knows
> Head over heels
> Face in the dirt
> I have been pushing plow too long
> Let me reap what I've sown

I listened to Freddy & Francine's *The Briar Patch* Friday afternoon during my drive down to Prosser to catch my friends' act at Brewminatti. Once again, "8 Pages" just kicked my hindquarters. The song is a vocal *tour de force* about enduring (and deserving) the worst kind of breakup.

> She wrote me 8 pages just to say
> She don't love me, she don't love me
> She wrote me 8 pages just to say
> She don't love me, she don't love me
> Any more

As the song concluded, I thought, "That would be so cool if they would do that song tonight! But what are the odds?"

About a zillion to one… but what the heck do I know?

Bianca Caruso and Lee Ferris are Freddy & Francine, and Friday night they told the story of their band and their off-

and-on-and-off-and-on-again relationship by taking the audience on a tour through their fifteen-year musical history.

Now in the eighth week of their current tour, they had tired of their conventional sets and decided three nights ago in Sisters, Oregon, to revisit some of their older material in upcoming shows… hence their inspired rendition of "8 Pages," received with wild enthusiasm by the sixty or so patrons of Marty Taylor's listening room in Washington's wine country.

Bianca peppered the two-hour show with engaging repartee about the duo's romantic history. Two of their first three discs (*The Briar Patch* and *The Forest and the Sea*) were written while they adamantly eschewed legendarily band-killing romantic entanglement—all the while incessantly penning love songs in close proximity. The irony in retrospect is deep, not to mention entertaining.

The inevitable happened, naturally—and their second album was recorded while delving into love… and breaking up the band. A three-year cold-turkey hiatus resulted in *Gung Ho*… which cemented their resolve to seek couples therapy and ultimately do the deed.

The couple married a year ago.

> I was a fool I couldn't see it through
> All of your scheming ways
> Have brought me to my knees
> You didn't mind
> Bringing me down
> You would have left me to the dogs
> If it suited you so

The story behind "8 Pages" is particularly entertaining. Secretly hoping that Lee would break up with his then-girlfriend, Bianca was surprised when Lee came to her with the news that he had been dumped... by post. The scenario was so funny—and gratifying—that Bianca suggested they turn it into a song. A few days later, when they debuted the number live, who should be in the audience but Lee's ex? That was definitely "all she wrote," as they say.

> Because you're selling me
> A story
> In my dreams
> That I can hold on to
> And let it go
> And never know I could be so true
> So walk the walk
> And talk the talk
> And make me a sad man

I've seen Freddy & Francine perform several times, and consequently expected a good show—but what a treat to get this semi-autobiographical look at many of their older songs and hear the backstories.

The evening was not unlike *Springsteen on Broadway*. It was "all true," as Bianca often pointed out... but it was storytelling, too. Just like the songs themselves.

> She wrote me 8 pages just to say
> She don't love me, she don't love me
> Any more

And what is the truth?

As Lee remarked in response to one question from the audience about "8 Pages," that's up to you to decide.

■

Southside

1981, spring, Seattle, Washington.

I'm culling through the second-hand collectible singles bin at Cellophane Square off The Ave in the U District.

A sophomore dormie at the University of Washington, I have a roommate (and a bunch of other friends) who is absolutely nuts about Bruce Springsteen. Through conversations and bits of news I pick up from fanzines and things I overhear at record shops, I have gleaned that there's this sort of Jersey Shore all-star band called Southside Johnny and the Asbury Jukes that some wags describe as Springsteen's shirt-tail.

The Jukes have released a few albums since their recording debut in 1976—but good luck finding them on the West Coast. Southside is still flying well under the radar... and always will, really.

And then I find an unexpected gem: a single of "Trapped Again," from 1978's *Hearts of Stone*, co-written by Springsteen, "Southside" Johnny Lyon, and "Miami" Steve Van Zandt (later to be known as "Little Steven"). I return to my dorm and roomie like a conquering hero with spoils of war.

Over the years, at Cellophane, 2nd Time Around, and Mount Olympus, I would continue my quest to track down Southside's albums. Probably a decade would pass before I'd manage to find a shrink-wrapped new release. A number of the used discs I'd purchase would be discarded radio-station promo LPs. I would eventually catch the act at Parker's in Shoreline—and dance a little with Michelle Noland, a former bandmate from those college days.

Johnny and Jukes have recorded a lot of fine music over the last forty years, with a variety of lineups—but the magic produced by the chemistry between Southside Johnny, Miami Steve, guitarist Billy Rush, and the Miami Horns proved impossible to beat. *Hearts of Stone*—mostly penned by Van Zandt, who also produced the album—is often referred to as "the best album that Bruce Springsteen never recorded"—a description that is really unfair, despite the presence of three Springsteen contributions, the Horns, Miami Steve, and drummer Max Weinberg.

If anything, this album convinced Springsteen that he needed Van Zandt—and his skill with horn arrangements—as a fulltime E-Streeter. *Hearts of Stone* is simply a fine, fine soul-influenced disc of adult heartbreak which drives toward its apex of emotion at the end of the A side.

The fourth is the titular track, which eavesdrops on a telephone conversation between failed lovers.

> If there was something, baby, that I could do
> Something that would last, honey, I would
> But we all know, girl, especially you do
> How you can't return to your past, no

The chorus then subtly poses a question: Hearts of stone, yes—but toward whom? The voices at either end of that telephone line—or toward a unseen party in the background?

> I can't talk now, I'm not alone
> So put your ear close to the phone
> 'Cause this is the last dance
> This is the last chance for hearts of stone

The track that follows, Van Zandt's "Take it Inside"—an urgent call to internalizing and owning the pain of failed and failing love—helps answer that question.

> How bad do you want it?
> How hard do you try?
> You don't ask no questions
> You don't find out why
> As you watch your life pass you by

These are not lovers in the throes of moving on—they are tragic fools, codependents who simply can't let go, even though holding on is killing them.

Yet the pathos in Lyon's vocals—and the opening of Van Zandt's lyric—prevents us from passing judgment. How else do you expect fundamentally broken people to behave?

> You call my name
> And like a fool I'm back again
> And I'm watching you die girl
> A little at a time
> While I try hard pretending
> That I don't mind

We all survive by learning effective ways to cope. To be honest, Springsteen's early music—as powerful as it is, driven by its mythically epic scope—most often describes juvenile drama beyond its author's ken. Springsteen openly admits these days that he was writing about things he never experienced, nonetheless capturing an essence of truth as an outside (and keen) observer.

Forty years down the road, though, *Hearts of Stone* rings as authentic as ever—the real measure of classic soul.

■

E.B. White

Words, anyone?

As a writer (and critic) I was weaned on "Strunk & White." Anyone else who was likewise weaned knows that's the shorthand name for *The Elements of Style*, the collegiate handbook version of *The Chicago Manual of Style*. Where the Chicago manual is more about the finer points of prescriptive pedant detail, Strunk & White has more of an artistic bent to it—more interested in, well, style.

Strunk & White appealed to me, I think, precisely because of its faults, described by one detractor thusly: "The book's toxic mix of purism, atavism, and personal eccentricity is not underpinned by a proper grounding in English grammar. It is often so misguided that the authors appear not to notice their own egregious flouting of its own rules."

Au contraire.

The authors very much notice their own egregious flouting, I believe.

For it is in the flouting where art resides.

I confess to not having thought about White, who wrote for *The New Yorker* for fifty years, in a good long time. While re-reading Sheldon Vanauken's *A Severe Mercy* yesterday, a toss-off quote from E.B. White—about the "quiet disrespect of libraries"—caught my attention. Vanauken implied that this came from a poem of White's, which took me aback. White? *Poetry?*

I couldn't get the quote out of my head as the day progressed, and I went back to re-read the page several times. Finally, I remembered to Google the quote... and came up empty. I guess there's a good reason I didn't know that White wrote poetry!

Certainly more famous for *Charlotte's Web* and *Stuart Little*, he did publish a good bit of poetry... but he's so revered for his prose that not much of this poetry has surfaced searchably on the Internet. I couldn't believe that Vanauken would quote a White poem that I couldn't find. (Such is my respect for Vanauken, and such is my confidence in my search-engine prowess.)

So I went to hard-core Web sleuthing... and finally located Vanauken's quote in an archive.org-scanned transcription of a 1940 issue of *Harper's* magazine—which published White's lengthy poem "One Man's Meat," which title White would later co-opt for a collection of essays.

The poem is a screed against the insanity of war, into which America had not yet been plunged, though the writing was on the wall by mid-1940. And this is the immediate context of Vanauken's quote. I quote at length:

> Books are their weapons,
> strange as that may seem—books, ideas,
> The same old swords but brighter now
> For having shown themselves imperishable.

> First of course books must be burned;
> This tempers them and makes them hold their edge.
> The enemy will take care of all that—
> I mean the book-burning. The fires
> Will soon be set; a day must come
> And you will smell it in the air,
> the unmistakable aroma of charred books.
>
> This happens when someone comes along
> Who hates and fears the irritant of Truth,
> The quiet disrespect of libraries.
> These old burnt books
> If only the incendiaries knew it
> Are like burnt pastures in the spring, cleansed,
> Ready for the new growth pushing through.
>
> It's never hurt yet, this burning of the books;
> The pages burn all right—words, songs, conclusions
> The dots and commas, the immediate dream;
> But when the fire cools there yet remains
> The fine imperishable ash. Young man
> Fear not the destroyer and the flame; Truth laughs at these.
>
> Fear only your own mind
> Where Truth, neglected, can so soon abort.

"All that I hope to say in books," White once commented, "all that I ever hope to say, is that I love the world."

Does this poem fragment sound like it was written by a soul which loved our world?

Why, yes, it does, to me. Because it comes from a heart that does not fear enemies; or rather, from a heart that has more confidence in Truth than it does in the strength of tyranny. A fine, fine thought for this—or any other—day.

It's a pity that the full text of "One Man's Meat" does not appear in readable form on the Web, or in print. So, flaunting, I suppose, the finer details of copyright law, I will leave you with these further excerpts:

> Things must be right if anything's to grow.
> O spark unquenchable, ember that will not cool,
> O youth if only I could make you see: This is your sword.
> This is your double-bitted ax,
> This is your miracle of gasoline chemistry—
> Books seem so ineffectual beside a tank; Nevertheless,
> Your enemy fears them in his heart
> He knows they'll find his heel at last.
>
> …
>
> Young man, advance! Stand here! Stand so!
> I shall instruct you where to go.
> I give you this bright western star
> To be your armored motor car;
> I give you songs old poets made
> New forged into a stainless blade,
> (Truth, however hard to bear, Will guard your rear).
> I give you Tolerance and Mirth,
> Love of rain and the wet earth
> (Without these you must not go forth).
> Wear Justice handy in your belt.
>
> …

Your secret thoughts, quick to wander
Will be your commander;
This is the gist of our attack,
This is our strength, our cause.
Our victory. Young man, be brave!
It is yourself that you must save.

■

The Council of Elrond

I recently received a notification that my name had surfaced in some German scholar's thesis about the cultural impact of Peter Jackson's *Lord of the Rings* movies.

While I was on the World Wide Web checking out that thesis and other brainy things, I discovered a transcript of a 2010 lecture by Tolkien scholar Tom Shippey concerning Tolkien's attitude about the artform of film. I pretty much had to guffaw as I read, given Shippey's rather gruff treatment of ol' Tollers.

To very briefly recap, without getting all technical and quotey about the Legendarium and its scribe, cuz I've done plenty of that elsewhere over the decades…

At one point after the rights to *Rings* had been sold, a film company submitted a script to Tolkien for his comment. Well, he pretty much bled over the whole thing. Finally, exasperated, he noted that the "rules of film" shouldn't be all that different to those of other narrative art, and any writer with half a noggin should be able to craft a script that didn't murder the spirit of the source material. (That's a paraphrase, but a pretty good one.)

Well, as I've done myself in many a lecture, Shippey pretty much ripped J.R.R. a new one over that. "The rules of narrative art?" he scoffed. "What did Tolkien know of observing the rules of narrative art?"

Note that this is not a criticism of Tolkien's literature. Quite the opposite. Shippey and I agree that the greatness of *The Lord of the Rings* lies, in very fact, in Tolkien's refusal to conform to narrative conventions.

This is a subject I wrote about extensively in 2004's *Peter Jackson in Perspective* (still in print), my analysis of how Jackson's vision of Middle-earth departs from Tolkien's.

The Old Forest and The Scouring of the Shire aside (both of which I discuss at length in *Perspective*), the greatest single instance of Tolkien's maverick style is The Council of Elrond.

I'll just let Shippey's words, not available in print, speak for themselves. While I've mentioned the topic in lectures, I haven't written about it previously... but Shippey dissects it well enough!

> There it is, Chapter 2 of Book 2 about rather more than half way through the volume, and it's a record of a committee meeting. And it's about... oh,... 20,000 words long!
>
> I tried to count up how many speakers there are, and I always get a different answer because it is so many. And many of them are actually introduced for the first time. I make it that there are over 20 speakers there if you include people who are introduced inside Gandalf's own narrative! You've got lots of speakers, some of them quite new, some of them quite unimportant. There are figures there who speak and take part in the discussion and do nothing else at all in the whole of the sequence!

One other thing that I have to say: I've been to many committee meetings, many, many committee meetings, and I reckon I know who is a good chair and who is not. And Elrond is a terrible chair; he lets the meeting get completely out of hand.

If I had been Elrond I'd have said, "Look, this meeting has three points to decide: one, is the hobbit's ring the One Ring? If it is, what are we going to do about it? And once we decide what to do about it, we've got to decide who is going to do it. Right. Item one on the agenda: Gandalf let us have your report…"

But, you know, instead we get Gloin telling us the history of the Mines of Moria. (Gimli doesn't speak. Again, slightly odd since he is going to be a character later on.) And Boromir tells us about Gondor and Gandalf says what he did on his holidays, and the whole thing fumbles along and Legolas says, Oh we lost Gollum, and… anyway, as Jackson rightly said, "That would just stop the movie dead! So we can't do that!"

Take that, Tolkien.

■

Ben-Hur

Misuk and I watched *Ben-Hur* on Christmas day.

"Ben-Hur?" asked my sister, Elane. "Seriously?"

If *Die Hard* can be called a "Christmas movie," well, sure! *Ben-Hur* is subtitled "A Tale of the Christ," after all, and it begins with the birth of Jesus, taking nearly ten minutes of wordless running time setting up the proper context for understanding the journey of Judah Ben-Hur.

Along for Judah's ride, as General Lew Wallace's novel and William Wyler's 1959 film have it, is Balthasar of Alexandria, one of the "wise men" who followed a star to find the "newborn king."

This marks the third time I've written about *Ben-Hur* this year, having reviewed the Fathom Event 60th Anniversary screenings at Easter as well as having written a Wonderstruck essay about destiny around the same time. But a movie review doesn't really allow the room to talk about the kinds of detail that struck me during my latest Blu-ray trip through the film.

"The race isn't over, Judah!" exclaims Messala as he lies dying in the wake of the spectacular chariot race. You'd naturally think of that stunning set piece as the climax of the movie; but Messala is right: It is not. The central conflict of the film is not Judah's struggle with his boyhood Roman pal; it is his struggle with his own self.

As Judah and Esther leave the Valley of the Lepers and Judah despairs of what he has learned there, they come once again across Balthazar as he joins a throng crossing a stream to hear Jesus preach. The mage has finally found the man he knew that the Bethlehem child would become: the Messiah, the Son of God.

Esther is also drawn to Jesus and joins Balthazar to hear Jesus preach his famous Sermon on the Mount.

Judah is not so drawn; instead, he is preoccupied with disappointment, loss, bitterness, rage, and plots of recrimination. He has no time for messages of peace and love.

Wyler's staging of this sequence is simply remarkable. Jesus is drawing crowds unto himself on the far side of a stream. Bridges span the shallow glen down which the stream wanders, setting up imagery that will be echoed in the film's closing shots; but all of Judah's deliberation takes place on the near bank.

After Judah has "chosen sides," as it were, the camera jumps over the stream to join the crowds at Jesus' feet. From there, we can see Judah continue his lonely, solitary way upstream; and over Jesus' shoulder, we can sense the Savior's eyes tracking not the crowd before him, but that lone and wandering sheep across the valley.

Wyler then proceeds to cut back and forth over Judah's shoulder and Jesus' shoulder, making it clear: Judah, in his isolation, ironically has no room for what Jesus has to offer; and Jesus, beset by a host of followers, would much rather have the company of the one who rejects him.

The detailed composition of these shots is astounding. On anything less than a forty-inch screen, I doubt you would even notice Jesus or Judah in the backgrounds of these shots; but on the big screen, or on a very large home TV screening Blu-ray HD, the intentional parallelism is hard to miss.

The producers even chose one of the shots over Jesus' shoulder as a "lobby card" image to promote the movie. Just to the right of Jesus' right shoulder is a lone tree, with a tiny lone figure standing to the right of the tree, looking across the gulf toward Jesus. That's Judah Ben-Hur.

In the final shot of this sequence, as we watch along with Jesus, Judah turns away one last time and strides headlong into the flock of sheep near the bridge, causing them to scatter.

What attention to detail.

Wyler: what a master.

Wonderstruck. Yippee-ki-yay.

■

Friedkin

Wonderstruck by who? you may well ask.

You may not know his name, but if you pay attention to movies at all, you almost certainly know his work: *The Exorcist*, *The French Connection*, *To Live and Die in LA*. You may even be familiar with *Blue Chips*, a collegiate basketball drama starring Nick Nolte and Shaq.

I stumbled across a recent interview with Friedkin on the Netflix series *The Hollywood Masters*, a short-format interview program in which film critic Stephen Galloway of *The Hollywood Reporter* sits down with legendary actors, producers, and directors. The chats, filmed before a live audience, are edited down into roughly half-hour segments.

I know first-hand how difficult it is to get anything meaningful out of a half-hour interview with an artist, even if you are well prepared and are familiar with the artist's body of work. But I struck gold with this Friedkin interview. For whatever reason, Galloway is really in his element in this one, pushing and prodding Friedkin on various points of artistic style and even the moral implications of the art.

When Friedkin says, for instance, that he was glad he never met Orson Welles because he "heard that he was a miserable son of a bitch," Galloway points out that the same could be said of Friedkin. To which Friedkin good-naturedly agrees.

Friedkin's relationship with cinema is so similar to mine—and to that of many others, I imagine. When he was seventeen years old, he says in the interview, "it was just entertainment to me, nothing to do with 'cinema' or art or anything like that." But then he attended a revival-house screening of Welles' *Citizen Kane*.

"I was just stunned by the experience," Friedkin still glows, some sixty years later. "I first experienced film as art." Justifiably so, even if audiences today can't find the same wonder in *Kane*. "Everything about it is as well done as can be done," he rightly points out. "Acting, writing, direction, cinematography, editing, the design—everything." Roger Ebert taught frame-by-frame seminars on the film for good reason. It is a masterpiece of the artform.

And so Friedkin's life turned. Movies became not just a pastime but a passion. And then a hard-won career.

"I don't have any rules," he says in response to Galloway's query about his creative process. "First, I don't want answers. I don't want a film to give me answers, only questions." It's a curious assertion, given that his films are not open-ended enigmas like those of the Coens or of contemporaries like Kubrick.

With his most financially successful film, *The Exorcist*, he points out that he does not find the film "dark" because in the end "the girl is saved." I have a hunch, though, that what Friedkin is talking about is the creative process itself, not the film proper. For instance, how did he manage to successfully deliver *The French Connection*, a pretty harrowing experience for all involved? "Total belief that nothing was gonna go wrong," he says, "that I could pull this thing off; and it was only that faith, that belief, and my belief in my colleagues—that they could pull this off with me."

So Friedkin's process is a great leap of faith into the unknown each time out; he doesn't want assurances that he will succeed. He wants something more challenging. After all, he observes, "we have no control over our fate."

Hence his 1977 film *Sorcerer*, about which I have previously written. The film is a reworking of the French thriller *The Wages of Fear* and tells the story of four desperate men individually trapped in a tiny, obscure South American town. The only way out for each of them is to attempt a hazardous transport of unstable nitroglycerin over mountain passes—with time of the essence.

In a way, the film is a metaphor for the creative process, not unlike Coppola's *Apocalypse Now!*, itself adapted from the European novel *Heart of Darkness*. "You did *Sorcerer* and it failed," observes Galloway. "It was a flop," he adds bluntly. "What happened?"

Friedkin takes no offense. "I have no idea," he honestly assesses. "This is the film of which I am most proud, and it was dead." With Friedkin's track record and reputation, with studio support, with star Roy Scheider—who was box-office gold—and with a wide release, the film should have taken off. But neither critics nor audiences got on board.

I would agree with Friedkin. I saw the film in the theater in 1977, and it had the same effect on me that *Citizen Kane* had on him. Despite the fact that I'd been raised on David Lean and Robert Wise, I had no idea that movies could be like

Sorcerer. "I wouldn't change a word of this film," says Friedkin, "or a shot." Absolutely.

The film was rehabilitated in 2014, and now, forty years after its release, enjoys a critical reception as an "overlooked masterpiece."

I can say the same for this interview with Friedkin, easily lost in a sea of otherwise ho-hum film chats. Friedkin acknowledges that *Sorcerer* is even "about something," that it does try to present the kind of answers he doesn't like in films.

It's "about the mystery of fate," he says.

So fitting. That Friedkin's fate as an artist would turn so fatefully and inexplicably on a failed film about fate.

I think he really is looking for answers.

■

Michael Kamen

I randomly played back tracks from my film score collection on my MP3 player the other day, and the first one up was the opening theme to the Tom Hanks-produced mini-series *From the Earth to the Moon* (1998).

The program tells the story of the various Apollo moon missions, taking unusual narrative angles not previously covered in other NASA-related movies and shows. Hanks introduces each episode with a thoughtful monologue, followed by sixty minutes of excellent writing, direction, and performances.

Many of my favorite actors did some of their best work in this series: Lane Smith, Nick Searcy, Dan Lauria, David Andrews, Carey Elwes, Stephen Root, Rita Wilson, Sally Field, Bryan Cranston, Tony Goldwyn, Adam Baldwin, Jo Anderson, Mason Adams, Mark Harmon, Joe Spano, Ted Levine, Dave Foley, JoBeth Williams, Peter Scolari, Peter Horton.

So where does Michael Kamen come in? He wrote the music for the show's opening theme—and what a stirring theme it is. It evokes Copeland's *Fanfare for the Common Man* or *Also Sprach Zarathustra* (the *2001* theme) in its brassy instrumentation, immediately and simultaneously conjuring both the human and divine scope of the Apollo endeavor. It concludes with barely perceptible notes that linger for well over thirty seconds, echoing the heartbeat of the universe—the "music of the spheres," as it were.

The images that play behind Kamen's theme during the series' opening credits include JFK's famous speech: "We choose to go to the moon— We choose to go to the moon in this decade, and do the other things, not because they are easy, but because they are hard."

For reasons that you might well guess if you knew my late wife Jenn, *From the Earth to the Moon* was one of her very favorite pieces of filmed entertainment. Several times over the course of her long illness, we re-watched this series and cried through many of its scenes—and it's hard for me not to be overcome with tears when I think of her own impossible mission… and our choice to see it through to the end, together, not because it was easy—but because it was hard.

As Kamen's score played over my speakers, the tears came again. And in my mind, I saluted Michael Kamen, Tom Hanks, all those actors, JFK, and the NASA faithful portrayed in the series.

And I again took my hat off to Jenn. Lord, but she was brave.

■

Jesus of Montreal

Back before I actually became a film critic, I somehow managed to get myself on publicist Nancy Locke's "influencers" list, which gave me periodic access to advance press screenings.

Most often, for whatever reason, the screenings for which I received invitations were Orion Films releases. I saw numerous wonderful films this way at Seattle's legendary Seven Gables theater—films like *The Purple Rose of Cairo*, *Babette's Feast*, and... *Jesus of Montreal*, which was released in 1989.

In the same way that *Babette's Feast* unexpectedly broke my face—I discovered after the screening that I had been smiling nonstop for ninety minutes, and my face wasn't used to it—*Jesus of Montreal* broke my mind. I'm not sure that any film I've seen since has struck me as so intelligently literary.

The literature in question in this film, of course, is the Bible. The plot is about a group of unknown actors who revitalize a summer-tourist passion play in Montreal—but director Denys Arcand's script also sets up Lothaire Bluteau's Daniel Coulombe (who plays the role of Jesus in the passion) as a reverse type of Jesus.

Everything that swirls around Coulombe plays out in a sort of blow-by-blow recapitulation of the ministry of Jesus. In this case, it's ministry through theater.

The film had me from the first scene. During the closing of a harrowing stage performance, a woman says of the male star, "I want his head." What a strange line; my literature-degreed brain perked up.

Then, at a post-performance reception, a gaggle of self-important art critics swarm to fawn over the actor... who's having none of it. When one wag declares, "You're the finest actor of your generation!" he spies Coulombe in the crowd.

"Excuse me," he demurs. "*There's* a good actor."

And it strikes me. Holy cow: This is a John the Baptist / Jesus relationship!

Was it a stretch for me to read this into such simple staging and efficient lines? Perhaps. But that's what lit majors do. They read into the text as they read.

But in this case, I was absolutely on the right track. Arcand's script and story are rife with such parallels: the adulteress, the pornographer, and the skeptic whom Coulombe calls as disciples; the corrupt TV commercial audition tables that a furious Coulombe overturns; the silver-tongued lawyer who takes Coulombe to a high tower and offers him the world... in exchange for his soul; the well-meaning followers who decide that the best way to memorialize their friend and savior is to form a corporation—"but only if we remain faithful to his ideas."

And this is all without even considering the content of the passion play itself, which of course tells the story of Jesus' death in a compellingly arresting (if controversial) fashion.

Or what the story presents: a stirring vision of the impact that someone like Jesus can have in the lives of ordinary people—people who need peace, patience, understanding, compassion, and love, people who need a heart of flesh instead of a heart of stone… or people who simply need eyes to see.

We may quibble over the "historicity" of the Man; but it seems that even atheists like Arcand understand that the Christ—and what he stood for—has the power to transform lives.

But here's the really crazy thing about this Oscar-nominated film: You can't watch it anywhere.

A few years back, I tracked down a multi-region DVD on the international market, so Misuk and I were able to watch the film last night.

But thirty years after it left theaters, the film does not appear on a single online streaming service… and a legit copy of the DVD will cost you $80 on Amazon.

Critics in the Toronto International Film Festival, Wikipedia tells us, "ranked the film second in the Top 10 Canadian Films of All Time in 1993 and 2004 and fourth in 2015."

But you can't watch it.

How strange is that?

Wonderstruck.

■

Tupelo Bar

> Mike was right when he said I'd put up
> A fight to be someone
> A fight to be me
> But see now I'm down
> Under the pavement
> Of capital ills and lowercase people

"Capital ills and lowercase people." Wow. How terribly relevant.

It's not often when you can dig twenty-odd years back into a band's repertoire and find a track that's been as consistently relevant as Switchfoot's "Company Car" from 1999.

Can we still party like it's that year?

> As time rolls by my dreams have become
> That which is attainable
> Not what I'm looking for
> I've got the company car
> I'm the one swinging at two below par

"That which is attainable": not very inspiring, is it? Not very Quixotic, quite literally. Instead of tilting at windmills—"not because it is easy, but because it is hard," to steal from JFK—we tilt back a pint of two of the foamy.

Ouch. Guilty, and charged.

Jenn and I had many a laugh over the years at that chorus. Courtesy of The Proclaimers, she had learned that Elvis hailed from Tupelo, Mississippi, so given the context she reasonably heard the lyric, "I'm the one swinging at Tupelo Bar," rather than "two below par." Yes, it's entirely reasonable for a swinger to drive his company car up to some high-class nightspot to boogie the night away with a roomful of Elvis impersonators… or fiddle while Rome is burning.

Haven't we all just sort of been swinging at Tupelo Bar for quite some time?

And who's to blame for that?

> Hey, I'm the king of things
> I've always despised
> I'm the ginger-bread man
> Who got eaten alive
> I'm half-baked, I'm fake

I could go on; but do I need to?

I think we all used to be optimists and dreamed big. Then life happened, and we got old. Flabby. Satisfied with less. Comfortably blah.

I credit Switchfoot for not simply continuing to "add to the noise" as they sang a few years later—for eventually opting out of the system that perpetuates "capital ills," and instead, for the last decade or so, consistently (and very Jesus-ly) siding with "lowercase people."

It's not everyone who can find oneself swinging at Tupelo Bar… and decide to stop hanging with all the impersonators.

Time to check out, maybe, yes?

∎

Thresholds

> thresh·old /ˈTHreSH‚(h)ōld/ noun: the magnitude or intensity that must be exceeded for a certain reaction, phenomenon, result, or condition to occur

One image that the word naturally conjures is a doorway: As you cross from one side to the other, you pass the threshold; existentially, we think of transitioning from one state to another—and often say, "Now there is no going back."

I ran into a friend today who has been out of town for a while. Her father had died suddenly, and she went to be with family for a time.

"It has been a strange enough year, hasn't it?" I remarked.

"Yes, it has," she agreed. "We lost two fathers and two grandfathers in just four months. And then, of course, there's Covid-19."

I could really only shake my head in condolence and smile weakly. But a thought popped into my head. I dismissed it and turned to walk away; still, something said, "No, this is not a random thought."

I turned back. "Did you ever listen to the Moody Blues?"

She immediately covered her eyes, gasped, tore her mask from her face, then quickly stepped three paces away. "I'm sorry," she said. "I just…"

"Some Moody Blues lyrics just popped into my head," I explained. "Words from one of Graeme Edge's poems." I quoted the bit that had come to mind.

> As new life will come from death, love will come at leisure.
> Love of love, love of life, and giving without measure
> gives in return a wondrous yearn of promise almost seen.

"Threshold of a Dream," I cited.

She wasn't crying, but she was clearly moved and raised her hand to her face once more before bringing her mask up again.

"*To Our Children's Children's Children* was the first album I ever bought," she said.

Grandfathers. Fathers. Children.

Live hand in hand—and together we'll stand on the threshold of a dream.

∎

Albert Lewin

As a fifty-eight-year-old student of film I certainly should have seen one of Albert Lewin's six produced motion pictures by now—*The Moon and Sixpence* (1942) or *The Picture of Dorian Gray* (1945), at least.

Thanks to my "cine-pal" correspondence with former colleague and filmmaker Nate Bell, I have now seen Lewin's *Pandora and the Flying Dutchman* (1951)... and I must say I was enthralled.

Nate and I first crossed paths in the Faith & Film Critics Circle somewhere around the turn of the century (we can say that now!), and as I recall I recruited him to contribute reviews to *Hollywood Jesus*, where I was Managing Editor for over a decade.

We have only met in person a couple of times, and one of those was for a highly memorable screening of Andrew Dominik's arty Western *The Assassination of Jesse James by the Coward Robert Ford* (2007) in Los Angeles. Nate has gone on to write and direct his own award-winning short films, and thanks to social media platforms we have managed to stay informed about what the other has been up to.

Recently, we began a film-exchange program. One of us sends an obscure but impressive title to the other on DVD or Blu-ray, and when the film is returned it is accompanied by another.

Knowing my taste in slow-paced, literate films such as Dominik's *Assassination*, I imagine, Nate most recently sent me Lewin's *Pandora*. As the title of the film might indicate, it is a story steeped in mythos. Its primary themes—destiny, timelessness, divine justice, serendipity—all appeal to me tremendously.

Lewin's visual and storytelling styles are also quite striking. Critic Susan Felleman has compared Lewin's work to the paintings of Botticelli, and not merely for the similarity in mythological references in the work. Lewin takes his time with setting up scenes (such as when Reggie drunkenly fiddles with his pillbox before fumbling his fatality into his drink) and opts for *outre* compositions (such as when Pandora flings herself on the ground near a precipice so that Lewin's camera can capture, in deep focus, the crashing surf far below with Pandora's hair and beguiling visage juxtaposed in the foreground). Further, "Lewin commissioned original artworks, songs, and dances for his films, which are visually stylized and thematically elaborate." In *Pandora*, a gypsy tango and a show-off moonlit bullfight stand out in this regard. Few films take the time with such sequences that "fail to move the story forward" in the conventional sense. But Lewin understands that the effectiveness of a film lies not just in Spielbergian efficiency, but also in tone, mood, and heart.

The story is about an ill-fated romance of epic proportions set in an exotic Spanish fishing community. Everyone is in love with Pandora, a beautiful, idle socialite. When a mysterious schooner drops anchor offshore, an intense romance with the ship's equally mysterious captain ensues.

So the filmmaking aside, a couple of things about the film particularly struck me.

First, the film's romance has an expiration date attached. Pandora has already agreed to marry another paramour, and the date has been set. Her new suitor, Hendrick, also has a fixed date for setting sail... and it happens to be the same date.

The date is September 3, which also happens to be my birthday. "I don't believe in coincidences," says Hendrick during his first encounter with Pandora. You can bet all *that* got my attention.

Second, a secondary theme of the film asserts that certain things can only come back to you through death. Without giving the plot away, I can tell you that the film opens and closes with a focus on an early edition of *Rubaiyat of Omar Khayyam*. It has been loaned to Hendrick by the story's narrator, archaeologist Geoffrey Fielding, and Fielding muses on the strangeness of the book rebounding to him in the film's closing scene.

The thrust of that theme—how life can only move forward through death—is obviously of great import to me, if you know my history. The words of the *Rubaiyat* quoted in the film say it all:

> The moving finger writes; and, having writ, moves on: nor all thy piety nor wit shall lure it back to cancel half a line, nor all thy tears wash out a word of it.

■

Apophenia

> Sometimes people with this condition get feelings of revelation or ecstasies. Sometimes people find patterns or meaning where there aren't any.
>
> What does that have to do with me?
>
> Creativity and psychosis often go hand in hand.

That's a bit of dialog from *The Queen's Gambit*, a Netflix miniseries about a chess ingenue.

So for the purposes of this article, the board is set. Follow these moves…

I have written before of an extraordinary dream in which a friend whom I had not seen or talked to in quite some time was getting married. I was in the wedding party and had the strongest foreboding that this engagement was a serious mistake; when, after waking quite shaken, I discovered that my friend was indeed engaged to be married, I contacted her further to discover that she had just broken off the engagement because God had told her it was a mistake.

Random? Perhaps. And I could rattle off a hundred quotes about the significance (or lack thereof) of coincidence and serendipity. But the interaction of dreams with reality takes things to an entirely different level, and such things are not isolated incidences in my world.

A couple weeks ago I had another dream in which my old friend Stephanie came to visit because she had something important to tell me. I was too busy to talk and put her off several times, fully intending to listen when I had the chance. Eventually, she simply left because I wasn't paying attention. And I awoke alarmed.

Although I had known Stephanie since second grade, I'm sure I had not dreamed of her since we were in college. At that time, we had been out of touch several years after her family moved away—and I dreamed that I finally found her new phone number and that we reconnected. Literally *the next day*, we pulled up next to each other at a stop light near the University of Washington, and I did indeed get her new phone number and reconnect.

So when, after thirty-five years, I dreamed of her again, I thought I should call. When she answered the phone, I immediately told her why I had called. Stephanie replied, "Oh, Greg, I have so many things to tell you. Where do I begin?" Among other things, her ninety-plus-year-old mother had just passed away from Covid-19.

May I confess that I still, after these and other examples from my own life, tend to doubt the significance of dreams? My childhood inculcation trained me to be skeptical of revelatory claims and the religiously ecstatic experiences of others. And what's bad for the geese must also be bad for the gander, right?

So after talking with Stephanie about her mother, in whose home I had many times been a young guest, I sat down to watch an episode of *The Queen's Gambit*. Midway through the series, Beth Harmon has become a notorious prodigy, and a *Life* reporter visits her home for an interview. It drives toward this exchange.

A janitor taught you to play chess?

Beth: When I was eight.

I imagine it must have been such a distraction from life in such a depressing place. You must have been very lonely.

Beth: I'm fine being alone.

Do you imagine that you saw the king as a father, and the queen as a mother? I mean, one to attack, one to protect?

Beth: They're just pieces. And it was the board I noticed first.

The board?

Beth: It's an entire world of just sixty-four squares. I feel safe in it. I can control it. I can dominate it. And it's predictable. So if I get hurt, I only have myself to blame.

How interesting. Tell me, have you ever heard of something called apophenia?

Beth: No, what's that?

It's the finding of a pattern or meaning where other people don't. Sometimes people with this condition get feelings of revelation or ecstasies. Sometimes people find patterns or meaning where there aren't any.

Beth: What does that have to do with me?

Creativity and psychosis often go hand in hand. Or for that matter, genius and madness.

I have written elsewhere about the late Christopher Hitchens' assertion that those who find meaning in great coincidences only do so because they have rehearsed themselves to do so. Their minds have become hopelessly biased, so goes this point of view. I have also argued to the contrary, with Hitchens as a case study: that *failure* to find meaning in serendipity is often the result of a mind rehearsed to do so. Such a mind has *also* become hopelessly biased.

I find that I have, rather, *been rehearsed by the universe* to perceive patterns and meanings where others may not; and further, I believe that my mind was naturally *predisposed* to do so. I also think we are all innately so predisposed; but education, "maturity," busy-ness, and a fear of the implications erect a wall against such disposition.

"Fear of the implications?" you may ask. Well, yes. Absolutely. If seemingly random events are not random at all... then "the butterfly effect" is not just a metaphor. It's an earth-shattering reality. Absolutely everything we do matters—and matters tremendously. What are the consequences of a thoughtless act? Think *that* through for a moment.

So it's very possible that apophenia is not at all a disorder; instead, it may be the sign not of a *diseased* mind but of a *healthy* one. If believing so is madness, I don't care to be sane.

■

Merry Gentlemen

> Lynne Truss is an English author, journalist, novelist, and radio broadcaster and dramatist. She is arguably best known for her championing of correctness and aesthetics in the English language, which is the subject of her popular and widely discussed 2003 book, *Eats, Shoots & Leaves: The Zero Tolerance Approach to Punctuation*.

So says Wikipedia. For nearly twenty years, word nerds have devoured Truss' witty volume on the vagaries of misplaced or absent punctuation. The title comes from a student's description of a panda whom, the student wrote, "eats, shoots & leaves."

The Oxford comma argument and inappropriate ampersand usage aside, the student is convinced, apparently, based on the punctuation, that the panda does *three* things: first dines; then shoots (whether that's a gun or some sexual or drug reference is unclear); and finally departs. The leaving would be understandable whether a sexual liaison *or* an assassination were underway, and both departures would be rather hasty, we imagine. And in both cases, the preliminary meal is puzzling.

What the student *meant* to write (and did in fact say, despite the mispunctuation) was that the panda's diet is varied. But the misapplied comma wreaks a very different effect than the one intended.

218

Every Christmas, I am reminded of Truss' book. Or, rather: My Christmas musings about punctuation predated Truss' book, but the tome's high profile elevated the internal justification for my annual holiday chafe. All boats rise on the same tide, as they say.

Thanks to the obscure language of many traditional carols (and the often stilted language associated with rhymed lyrics) we all regularly sing songs that we simply don't understand. The most glaring example of this is, of course, "Auld Lang Syne," which everyone gets weepy over without ever understanding why. (*I* won't tell you why. If you want to know, you know where Google is.)

But one sneaky devil that goes remarkably unnoticed is the song we generally refer to as "God Rest Ye Merry Gentlemen," as much a disservice to its long-forgotten author as to grammarians world-wide… because, as Lynne Truss points out in such cases, we have simply gotten either lazy or punctuation-shy; that is, latterly, we don't want others to criticize our punctuation… so we *leave it out entirely*.

But the opening line of that song does indeed beg a comma, and the placement makes all the difference.

Consider first the punctuation which first appeared in print and which Dickens cribbed in his *Christmas Carol*: "God rest ye, merry gentlemen. Let nothing you dismay."

Other grammatical quibbles aside, this reading would translate in contemporary English to something like: "Stay the way you are, happy dudes. Don't let anything disturb your calm."

The troubles with this reading are manifold.

First, it flies in the face of archaic usage of the verb "rest," or "continue in," which always requires an object (which may, granted, be implied); second, and most importantly, what do these happy dudes have to be dismayed about, if they are indeed already happy? They certainly don't seem to be in need of a reminder about Christian salvation. The Good News, in this scenario, seems rather superfluous.

If the dudes are already happy, why bother interrupting them?

But the dudes are *not* happy. That's why the song exists.

By contrast, the correct punctuation, which appeared later in print and then at some point vanished entirely, was: "God rest ye merry, gentlemen. Let nothing you dismay."

Again by contrast, this would translate today to something like, "Get your happy jones going again, dudes. Don't let hard times get you down." This makes *much* more sense out of the Good News which follows.

Again to translate: "It may be the darkest time of the year, but that's why we celebrate Christmas in this season! For God sent that little baby to get us all out of whatever mess in which we find ourselves. That's of great comfort, right? And reason to be joyful."

So now that I've ruined Pentatonix for you—they who avoid the comma controversy entirely and beg God to put a bunch of happy dudes to bed—still I say:

"Never mind me. Get your happy jones going again, dudes. Don't let me, or any of these hard times, get you down. God really *does* intend to get us out of this mess."

Whether it's Covid-19, presidential elections, or lousy punctuation.

■

Elf

Ed Asner turned to me, extended his hand, and said "Hi. I'm Ed."

> Oh, hello! You're probably here about the story. Elves love to tell stories. I'll bet you didn't know that about Elves.

So this was the deal: My arrival in Manhattan was delayed.

By the time my flight had circled JFK several times through a cloud of swirly-twirly gumdrops, I was running well over ninety minutes behind schedule. I was due that night for a press screening of New Line Cinema's Will Ferrell Christmas movie, *Elf*, and it was beginning to look a lot like Miss-mas.

In those days, fortunately, I traveled strictly carry-on, so I was able to immediately hail a taxi upon my arrival at the airport. The publicist promoting the film was tracking my travel and was waiting at the curb for me when I stepped out of the cab. The chartered bus holding the balance of the press corps was standing by for departure to the theater, so the publicist grabbed my bag and said she'd take care of check-in at the hotel. Off I was whisked to the bus.

During my days as a film critic, I did try to know as little about films as I could before I saw them; but this was ridiculous. Usually, I at least had time to change out of my travel clothes, grab a pre-screening bite to eat from the press reception lounge, and browse through the weekend's call sheet to familiarize myself with the players involved, the schedule of interviews, and what the next day's meal arrangements might be. None of that for *Elf*. I was off to the screening and had no idea what was up.

I also tended to keep to myself at press events. I found a good many reviewers overly chatty, only too eager to dish details about stars, plot points, or behind-the-scenes scandals. Everyone likes to be in-the-know, after all.

So having arrived by charter bus at the screening venue for the event, I truly went into *Elf* cold. Appropriate enough, right?

And what a delight that screening was! As we all know now, twenty years later, Jon Favreau directed Ferrell into a PG-rated anti-*Old School* Christmas classic, spreading Christmas cheer for all to hear.

End of story, right?

Hardly. The night was just beginning.

As the press was being herded back to the bus, the publicist, who had rejoined the group after dealing with my luggage at the hotel, remarked, "So are you excited about the party?"

"Party?" I responded.

Now, Ridley Scott had proposed the press screening of *Kingdom of Heaven* be held at a Scottish castle—an idea which was unfortunately nixed at the last minute because a couple high-falutin' film critics (get this) *didn't have passports*—

but nothing in my ten-year stint as a reviewer was gonna top *this* night.

The producers had arranged to throw a private Christmas party for the press corps in the penthouse suite of the Empire State Building… with the cast of the film.

Now, by "cast of the film," I took the publicist to mean "one or two of the cast members, and probably the lesser-known ones at that."

But no. When I stepped off the gleaming elevator and into the decked-out penthouse observation room, with the Manhattan skyline spread before us beyond the buffet tables, lights, and Christmas decorations, what to my wondering eyes should appear but, yes, the *entire* cast of *Elf*. James Caan, Will Ferrell, Mary Steenburgen, Zooey Deschanel, Faison Love, and others circling in the shadows. Probably producers and whatnot.

This was surreal.

By this time, of course, I wasn't starstruck by meeting celebrities. But ordinarily we met with them in very controlled circumstances, with publicists, reps, and handlers regulating how much one could talk with the stars. There certainly wasn't any personal chit-chat involved. (I did once share an elevator with Sean Bean at the Beverly Hills Four Seasons the night of the world premiere of *The Return of the King*, though, and we informally chatted a bit. He didn't feel compelled to be at the screening because he "had already seen the movie" and his scenes were being "held for the extended cut.")

But here I was grabbing a plate of cookies.

Elbow-to-elbow with Sonny Corleone... er, James Caan. Geez.

I'm not entirely sure what the point of the evening was. I imagine that the producers thought that the schmooze might yield slightly better reviews for the film; but how can one improve on a five-star experience? Maybe they were just giddy and wanted to share the good will.

In any event, I went over to the punchbowl, and a rather shortish rotund older gentleman turned to me, extended his hand and said, "Hi, I'm Ed."

Well, duh. It was hard not to recognize Ed Asner.

I was nonetheless stunned. What was Ed doing here? I figured I should know, so I was too embarrassed to ask Mr. Asner the obvious question.

A bit later I pulled one of my colleagues aside, perhaps Chris Monroe, and asked about Asner's presence. "He was Santa Claus! Didn't you recognize him?"

No—no, I hadn't. I was so caught up in the magic that is *Elf* that I wasn't processing the film at that level. I guess I was simply believing in Santa again, not thinking about the actors, Christmas Spirit buoying my evening. Sheesh.

I never did really converse with any of the stars at the party. It simply didn't feel "professional" to do so. A handful of us decided to leave the soiree early, but when we went down to hop back into the charter bus, it was nowhere to be found. Security at the now-shuttered Empire State Building wouldn't allow us back in, so we decided to hoof it to the hotel. After half an hour or so of wandering the streets of Manhattan in the cold, we hailed a cab and made it back to the hotel safe and sound.

But what a strange evening. I don't think any of us were aware of cinema history being made.

When I turned on the *Elf* episode of Netflix's limited series *The Holiday Movies That Made Us*, memories of that weekend in Manhattan came flooding back.

Buddy the Elf is a truly memorable and classic Christmas character—much like George Bailey, but without the dark edge.

Who better to share Christmas with than someone who "cares about everybody"?

Kinda like that Jesus guy.

■

Michael Mann

From an awards standpoint, Michael Mann picked a poor year to release his masterpiece *The Last of the Mohicans*.

In 1992, he was up against the juggernauts *Unforgiven*, *A Few Good Men*, *The Scent of a Woman*, *Glengarry Glen Ross*, and *The Crying Game*, amongst a few others, and Daniel Day-Lewis was coming off an Oscar win for his previous film, *My Left Foot*.

Release this film in any other year, and you'd likely have a slew of award nominations.

Or maybe not.

Mann rightly judged, probably, that audiences would have an easier time accessing the heart of this story through an emphasis not on Uncas, the hero of James Fenimore Cooper's novel, but on Nathaniel Bumppo—played with true method-acting gusto by Day-Lewis.

Still, the heart of this film is not really in the class- and culture-flouting romance between Bumppo and military brat Cora Munro; nor is it even in the relational dynamic of the orphaned Natty raised as brother to Uncas by the last surviving Mohican warrior, Chingachgook. The heart of this film is the fear of dying cultures.

The film's culminating conflict, after all, is between Chingachgook, who has just witnessed the last hope of his tribe, son Uncas, slain by Mohawk warrior Magua, and Magua—himself motivated by blood revenge, the lone survivor of the British slaughter of his Mohawk family, and fostered by the Huron.

These two men know a thing or two about culture clashes, thorough destruction of a way of life, and the pain of loss. They also learn the emptiness of vengeance.

That Chingachgook is played to perfection in the film by American Indian Movement revolutionary and legend Russell Means—wickedly wielding the "gunstock war club"—and that Magua is chillingly portrayed by now-legendary Native American actor Wes Studi in an Oscar-worthy supporting role simply adds to the gravitas of that final confrontation.

The film, quite frankly, is not just a cinematic-narrative and production-design masterpiece as well as a thing of visual beauty; it is also a socio-political commentary powderkeg.

Hawkeye, Uncas, Chingachgook, Magua, the Huron chief Sachem, the frontier settler Cameron family—even Cora and her sister—are all pawns in global forces beyond their control. France and England, and the American Indian nations themselves, jockey for power with little regard to either the immediate or long-term human consequences of their politics; and it's truly difficult to pick which party to the conflict behaves more despicably.

The film is heartbreaking.

Consider that there is no mercy for selfless sacrifice: Hawkeye is beaten with vicious coup when he walks unarmed into a

Huron camp; British officer Duncan Heyward is burned at the stake and mercy-shot when he surrenders his life in place of both Cora Munro and Hawkeye; and Alice Munro gives her life away to honor Uncas rather than grant Magua the grace of his would-be repentance from his blood oath.

But frankly, the film consistently breaks my heart because all these characters—in the face of the great beauty that was the American frontier and the great beauty that exists in the American wilderness, like the film's settings in North Carolina—succumb to the natural destructive instincts we have for self-preservation and revenge in the face of loss. "An eye for an eye leaves the whole world blind," Gandhi is supposed to have said. Michael Mann's film certainly makes a strong case for the sentiment.

But how could the world be any different?

The Last of the Mohicans does offer some insight into hope as well, if we choose to pay attention.

A Magua may be a threat today; but a Magua *does not come out of nowhere*. As Wes Studi said in interviews about the making of the film, he does not play Magua as a villain, even though his acts are indeed heinous; he plays Magua as a wronged party and motivated patriot.

Think about that a little. Magua is not so different from Chingachgook. Magua's motivation is not all that different from "Remember 9/11!"

Magua's leadership is not all that different from that of Adolf Hitler.

These motivations are completely understandable, and history is rife with them.

So today, while we deal the Maguas in our midst—while we may in fact *be* the Maguas in our midst—we also need to be thinking about the Maguas of tomorrow. Do we need more of them?

The answer to that question always starts with us. We can learn from history—and from art—or we can be doomed to repeat it.

Particularly at this time of year we are reminded that there is a better way than "an eye for an eye," that mercy triumphs over judgment, that the One who said, "Pray for your enemies" and "Blessed are the peacemakers" lived what he said. And his Apostles consistently interpreted his teaching and life to mean "as far as it depends on you, be at peace with all men."

> I have said these things to you, that in me you may have peace. In the world you will have tribulation. But take heart; I have overcome the world. (John 16:33)

You will find the reality of this broken world in *Mohicans*. But the film also may remind us that there are alternatives to embrace of such brokenness—that all things are possible with God, and that he wants so much more for us than we can ask or imagine.

∎

Zhivago

Do we all still remember that as recently as ten years ago we were still trying to rather forcibly export democracy to the Middle East?

So strange that so many of the very souls which were so gung-ho about the effort are now so very eager to abandon our own democratic institutions in favor of mob rule and "tribunals."

I suppose that the only way to truly appreciate the effect a work of art has had on oneself is to revisit it after fifty-some years. I first saw *Dr. Zhivago* when I was around six years old. The film opens with the orphaning of Yuri Zhivago at about four years old, and I distinctly remember identifying with his disorientation; his fascination with wind, snow, blowing leaves, ice, and branches tapping at the window in the night; and his awareness of both the bleakness and the beauty of the world. That both Yuri and I became poets is not terribly surprising.

I also grew up with an LP of Maurice Jarre's evocative soundtrack for the film. His use of many clanging cymbals in the context of musical dissonance made clear to me what the Apostle Paul talked about in I Corinthians 13.

I am quite sure that the romance, in which Yuri and Larissa Antipova repeatedly cross paths in an ill-fated destiny, also influenced my tendency to fall in love with girls and women and then keep having them re-enter my life years and decades later.

But the biggest impression the film made was its depiction of life in post-revolution Russia. Trading one set of blackguards for another did not seem like a terribly good bargain to my young mind—which has ever since appreciated the stability of an imperfect union over the shifting sands of rudderless chaos. The worst thing in the world, it seemed, would be to have some arbitrary bunch of yahoos deciding quite violently, and with prejudice, who are "enemies of the people" and dispensing justice accordingly. And with the cast of goons changing on a weekly or monthly basis. Sheesh.

Sorry, but as a citizen, I'm sticking with due process, rights of representation and appeal, and constitutional law and order. If I don't like the way our system works, I will do what I can to exercise my right to vote and legislate my way out of the mess—and trust in the system to self-correct, which it is very much designed to do every two or four years.

And as a pastor... well, I'm naturally still convinced that love triumphs over evil—that repaying evil with more evil is the worst possible choice.

I'm still choosing to follow the words of Jesus in the Sermon on the Mount over shrill, alarmist, and anonymous voices that are most definitely "clanging cymbals."

If you find yourself in need of love in the coming days or weeks, you know where to find me. I'll be sheltering in my own personal Varykino ice palace with my own personal Lara, determined to love through whatever days we might have left.

Like Yuri and Lara, we know what we stand for, and we aren't budging.

It's beautiful.

∎

Nuremburg

While a fictional feature film should never be confused with a historical document, movies can sometimes do a very good job of concisely summarizing a good deal of historical detail. *Judgment at Nuremburg* is not only one such film, but also captures what made the historical tribunal a concern to the legal community.

What it gets particularly right—and thus the concern—is the real Nuremburg trial's conclusion that justices, even Supreme Court justices, can be held legally accountable for allowing other branches of government to erode the rule of law. The precedent would be dangerous, so the reasoning went, because justices would be reluctant to serve.

That concern has, apparently, not proven valid. In America, at least, justices may turn out to be our most staunch patriots.

I find Stanley Kramer's film very balanced in its approach to the topic. His protagonist is played by Spencer Tracy as reluctant, dubious about passing judgment on fellow justices.

So viewers are not treated to a lot of posturing self-righteousness from Kramer or the American in the film with whom we most identify. Instead we get introspection, which is always healthy, and a dose of self-doubt.

Kramer's indictment comes from the mouth of one of the judges in the dock, the fictional Ernst Janning, played with stony coldness and authoritative guilt by Burt Lancaster. When Maximilian Schell's defense attorney starts badgering a Jewish witness to Nazi miscarriage of justice, Janning decides to put a stop to it by finally breaking his silence. What follows are lines from his monologue.

> I wish to testify about the Feldenstein case because it was the most significant trial of the period. It is important not only for the tribunal to understand it, but for the whole German people. But in order to understand it, one must understand the period in which it happened.
>
> There was a fever over the land, a fever of disgrace, of indignity, of hunger. We had a democracy, yes, but it was torn by elements within. Above all, there was fear, fear of today, fear of tomorrow, fear of our neighbors, and fear of ourselves.
>
> Only when you understand that can you understand what Hitler meant to us, because he said to us: "Lift your heads! Be proud to be German! There are devils among us, communists, liberals, Jews, gypsies. Once these devils will be destroyed, your misery will be destroyed."
>
> It was the old, old story of the sacrificial lamb.

That is to say, not just an ironic invocation of the Hebrew system of atonement for sins, but the Christian indictment of High Priest Caiaphas who basically suggested that Jesus should be killed in order to keep Rome from coming down on Judea.

If somebody has to go down, well, just find out who's most expendable.

What about those of us who knew better, we who knew the words were lies and worse than lies? Why did we sit silent? Why did we take part?

Because we loved our country. What difference does it make if a few political extremists lose their rights? What difference does it make if a few racial minorities lose their rights? It is only a passing phase. It is only a stage we are going through. It will be discarded sooner or later. Hitler himself will be discarded sooner or later.

Political expediency is always a risky gamble, especially when it comes to known sociopaths.

"The country is in danger." We will "march out of the shadows!" We will "go forward." Forward is the great password.

And history tells how well we succeeded, Your Honor. We succeeded beyond our wildest dreams. The very elements of hate and power about Hitler that mesmerized Germany mesmerized the world! We found ourselves with sudden powerful allies. Things that had been denied to us as a democracy were open to us now.

Newfound power and influence can be terribly seductive to the marginalized and threatened.

And then one day, we looked around and found that we were in an even more terrible danger. The ritual begun in this courtroom swept over the land like a raging, roaring disease. What was going to be a "passing phase" had become the way of life.

As Sean Connery's street cop in *The Untouchables* said, "Here endeth the lesson."

■

Jesus

I know what you're thinking.

Okay, I probably don't.

But I *do* know how a lot of people are likely to respond to my headline for this piece. I know because for all of my life I have been skeptical of filmed portrayals of Jesus, of their glaring anachronisms and at the very least unwitting racism, and of the oddly non-Semitic casts that fill these films. (Hollywood has had Jewish actors portray Indians more often than actual Jews.)

The other thing is that I am a snob.

I am a religion snob, and I am a film snob. I may not be as much of a religion snob as some other pastors, and I am definitely not as much of a film snob as the majority of my fellow critics; but I am nonetheless a snob. I generally find most practice of Christianity to be of the sort that Jesus said he'd like to spew out of his mouth in Revelation, and on the basis of artistic merit I generally want to hold my nose while watching films made for the "Christian audience."

Now, I generally rely on the Spirit of God to help temper my thoroughbred snobbery, and the Spirit is mostly successful; and, as I remarked to my wife when we sat down to watch some of *The Life of Jesus* on YouTube the other night, the Bible isn't going to be much help to us if we always come to it armed with our biases and our own sense of superiority. So I commended her choice of film not for its cinematic quality, whatever it might turn out to be, or because its makers had their theology and interpretation of Scripture all straight, but because this was one of those films where the narration and dialogue all come straight from Scripture—in this case, the Gospel of John.

And if you love Jesus, getting more Jesus straight from the words of Scripture is always a good thing.

So I won't detail what I think this production "got wrong," and I'm not about to catalog everything it got right. Having buried my snobbery for a couple days (or at least, hopefully, while writing this note), I'd rather just be wonderstruck at something I've never before gleaned from "The Last Supper," as the episode in Scripture is called.

Because I can be a snob, most of my recent insights into this passage have focused on things that others tend to "miss" when reading through John's lengthy account of the evening. Because, you know, if you notice things that other people miss, it makes you appear so much sharper. Am I right, or am I right?

But yesterday I noticed something that *I* had been missing. That I have *always* missed, for over five decades now.

Yes, we all know that Jesus said he was aware that Judas was going to betray him. According to John, who was sitting at Jesus' side during the meal, Jesus even told Judas, "Go, and do what you must."

But here's the thing.

Even though Jesus knew Judas was a "traitor," a "turncoat," a "Benedict Arnold," a "seditionist," or whatever term you might like to apply, Jesus still treated Judas the same as his other followers.

He still washed Judas' feet.

He still invited Judas to sit with him.

He still broke bread for Judas.

He still loved Judas.

Judas did what Judas had set his heart to do; but that did not change *Jesus*—whose goal, even in the face of betrayal and death, was still to minister and to serve.

Huh.

There are a lot of moving parts to events in our nation right now, and I would guess that 98% of Americans believe one of these two things: that they are acting right now to save the country from traitors; or that they are witnessing the lawless acts of traitors.

My, but what of lot of traitorous wretches are we Americans.

Some or all of those assessments are almost certainly true; and the courts, the news, social media, and your neighbors down the street are all trying to sort out who's who.

But for today, this is what *I* have learned.

If I want to be like Christ, even when I find a *bona fide* traitor I'm gonna minister and serve. And love the hell out of that traitor.

Now, if you want to ask me, "That all sounds well and good, Greg; but what in practice might that look like?"

I reply: Why don't you go to Scripture and see what Jesus has to say to you about that? He and his Spirit can be your guide much better than I.

∎

Robert Guiry

Jacob Sahms, writing at *ScreenFish*, recommended the latest Sandra Bullock film the other day.

The Unforgivable is on Netflix, and while I am not really a Bullock fan (per se), I am a Sahms fan. (We are both pastors and were colleagues in film criticism at one time. There's history there.) So I decided to check it out.

Toward the end of the film—almost at the very end, in fact—I thought, "Huh. This film really reminds me of one of my favorite indies from the early part of this century." *Steel City*, an excellent vehicle for the talents of the late, great John Heard.

The themes and structure of the two films are so similar, in fact, that after the credits for *The Unforgivable* started running I immediately flipped over to IMDb to see if *Steel City* were streaming anywhere. (It is: on Amazon Prime.)

As the poster for *Steel City* popped up on my screen, I literally said out loud, "I'll be damned." Which I'm not, of course; and neither are you. But such things do tend to pop out of my mouth from time to time thanks to the overdramatic enculturation of my youth. *Planet of the Apes* and all, you know.

There on the screen was the face of an actor I had just been watching on Netflix for the last two hours: not Sandra

Bullock (or John Heard), but supporting character actor Tom Guiry, who in *Steel City* played one of two warring brothers who struggle with their father's legacy. In *The Unforgivable*, he played Keith, one of two warring brothers who struggle with their father's legacy.

Now, I have probably seen ten thousand movies as an adult, and there is not one of those films as close in thematic content and story structure (not actual plotting, but story) to *The Unforgivable* as *Steel City*. That both should feature Tom Guiry in similar roles is... well, almost beyond believing.

It's not like Guiry is a household name, after all; nor does he have hundreds of films to his credit.

You might remember him from *Mystic River*, however... where he played one of two brothers who struggle with their father's legacy.

Yep.

All three films deal not only with sibling and filial issues but with miscarriages of justice... and perhaps-misguided attempts to shield those we love from the consequences of their actions.

I don't think Guiry's appearance in these films is an accident.

Wow. I'd dearly love to talk to this guy about his artistic choices. Something is really going on in his life.

Wonderstruck.

Equinox

Podcaster Andrew Hackett has been posting lists of his favorite films from the 1980s and 1990s the last couple of weeks. These decades were right in the wheelhouse of my years of pre-critic film study, so I have been greatly enjoying interaction with his lists.

Given his tastes, I was surprised that Alan Rudolph's *Equinox* (1993) did not show up on his list for that year... and even more surprised to learn that Andrew had not even *seen* the film.

As with many Rudolph films, the characters in *Equinox* inhabit stylized worlds that more resemble cinematic tropes than real life—and in *Equinox*, that is more true for Lara Flynn Boyle's Beverly than anyone. Her aim in life is to disappear into a facsimile of a favorite painting... in part because she and her friend Henry, among others, are so incapable of functioning even within a stylized "real world." The larger story concerns the tension between low-key Henry and his gangster doppelganger, who may or may not be his identical twin brother.

Equinox is a fascinating film. What's more fascinating is that, in this digital age, it's not widely available to stream. Right now, it's only available through iTunes. Further, it was never released on DVD, which explains how it has vanished from my personal library.

Other great films that are just as hard (or harder) to find:

The Sure Thing (1985), directed by Rob Reiner. The rom com that made John Cusack a star.

The Flamingo Kid (1984), directed by Garry Marshall. A really endearing and gentle family comedy with a great ensemble cast that includes Matt Dillon, Hector Elizondo, Bronson Pinchot, Fisher Stevens, and Richard Crenna.

Mindwalk (1990), directed by Bernt Capra (no relation, if you are wondering). Two hours of stunningly fascinating and challenging conversation between a politician (Sam Waterston), a physicist (Liv Ullman), and a poet (John Heard).

Seriously? We can't watch these films easily?

Wonderstruck.

Tolkien

Twenty years ago, Peter Jackson unleashed the opening salvo of his *Lord of the Rings* trilogy upon an expectant world… and he did not disappoint.

Yes, there was much quibbling over the specifics of his *Fellowship of the Ring* and his Middle-earth (and I was right in the thick of all that online chatter), but the consensus after just four years (much less after the last two decades) is that Jackson's is the best LotR we could possibly hope for.

Watching Steven Colbert's celebratory "LotR Rap," I was reminded how deeply I was embedded in the years between the initial release of *Fellowship* and the release of the Extended *Return of the King*. I ended up publishing hundreds of thousands of words about the films in my role as Managing Editor of *Hollywood Jesus*, and after my initial salvo was picked up by *The One Ring* (and ended up translated into Spanish and Swedish without my knowledge!) I went viral and became a Tier 2 international authority on all things Tolkien.

I would go on to publish three books on *The Lord of the Rings* and *Narnia*, and speak at Baylor and Notre Dame (amongst other places) as well as the Tolkien 50 conference at Aston University in England. My paper on cinematic fantasy at the 2005 Past Watchful Dragons conference was considered the touchstone of the event.

The culmination of it all, though, was really the 2004 One Ring Celebration in Pasadena. RotK had just won its barrel full of Oscars, and as I was an established and popular panelist on the Con circuit I was asked to present the top award at the closing night gala dinner. My late wife, Jenn, and I were hanging out backstage with Sean Astin, Billy Boyd, Dominic Monaghan, and Elijah Wood when Jenn began to feel quite ill. Vomiting all over Orlando Bloom really wasn't a good option, so we elected to retreat to our hotel... and I made my apologies to the organizers.

I ended up missing my biggest moment in the spotlight because my wife's comfort was more important.

I still think with fondness about that quiet moonlight stroll we enjoyed in gown and tux, however, as we slowly made our way arm in arm through Pasadena's gardens. It was as peaceful and elegant a night as we ended up sharing during our marriage. We did not know at the time that it was the initial throes of a twelve-year final illness that would ultimately take Jenn's life.

And it was just as well that the spotlight began to fade that night. Within eighteen months I was a full-time caregiver, and by 2007 I had bowed out of cinematic circles almost entirely. My last gig as a critic was a Disney invitation to cover the London Royal Premiere of *The Voyage of the Dawn Treader* in December 2010.

I am honored to have played a significant role in the media circus that was *The Lord of the Rings*. My essays and interviews with Jackson, Boyens, *et al* directly impacted the home-video Extended Edition of *The Return of the King*, and my book on

Jackson's films (still the only comprehensive critical study of the trilogy) remains in print after nearly twenty years. My work introduced me to a great number of wonderful people who remain good friends to this day.

I won't say the experience was "humbling," however. When I hear people say such things, I want to quote Inigo Montoya: "You keep using that word. I do not think it means what you think it means." One may feel fortunate to have had such unexpected and undeserved journeys… but humbling? No. Not really. "Humbling" is walking in the moonlight with your wife, instead of hosting a gala, because it's the right place to be.

Covering *The Lord of the Rings* was nothing but pure adrenaline-inducing excitement for a Tolkien nerd. A pleasure and a privilege to a part of history.

Wonderstruck.

■

The Railway Man

It's not every day that you tune in to Netflix and hear the fifth chapter of Paul's letter to the Romans quoted.

Years after it was filmed, and after having languished on my watchlist for months, *The Railway Man* finally graced my living room TV screen. Nominally starring Colin Firth and Nicole Kidman, and initially masquerading as a late-in-life romance, the film is actually a dramatization of the PTSD experienced by soldiers (British POWs and their Japanese overseers) who labored on the Burma railroad during World War II.

Conditions were appalling, and the treatment of the UK's POWs horrendous. The film spends a good deal of time recounting the POW experience of one Eric Lomax. So, while Lomax the elder is played by Mr. Firth, the real stars of the film are the younger actors who portray wartime Lomax and his fellows.

The film is bracketed by lines from the poem "The Clock of Man," written by the real Eric Lomax in his later years:

> At the beginning of time the clock struck one
> Then dropped the dew and the clock struck two
> From the dew grew a tree and the clock struck three
> The tree made a door and the clock struck four
> Man came alive and the clock struck five
> Count not, waste not the years on the clock
> Behold I stand at the door and knock

The final line is a reference to Revelation 3:20: "Behold, I stand at the door, and knock: if any man hear my voice, and open the door, I will come in to him, and will sup with him, and he with me." Lomax had ample opportunity to ponder the passage of time while imprisoned in isolation, and the poem he crafted was recitation therapy as he lay in the grip of PTSD terrors years later.

What really weighed on Lomax's heart, however, was the resentment he bore toward his captors. His longing was for that door to be opened and for Christ to enter in and heal. His story, naturally, and the film as a result, is rather saturated in the hope of the Gospel: hope for forgiveness and reconciliation.

The poem at the opening certainly pricked up my pastor's ears, as did a particularly ironic recitation of Psalm 23; but I was further flummoxed to hear a bit of Romans 5 included in background dialogue:

> Very rarely will anyone die for a righteous person, though for a good person someone might possibly dare to die.

The quote is from one of the key passages in Scripture about enemies being reconciled by the One who stands at the door and knocks. It's a pretty heady bit of theology to incorporate into any narrative, much less one about war crimes. But what really floored me is that I had just been reading that passage of Romans during my daily studies.

Further, the forty-year hard lessons of reconciliation that Lomax and his Kempetai interrogator learned bore a striking resemblance to the forty-year lessons of my own life. For a decade, I have been working on the following poem, "The Act of Graduation," about resentment toward the bullies of my childhood.

> Ron Buehler stands before me,
> vested, hatted, mustachioed.
> He's pushing fifty and so am I.
> We are both completely civil.
>
> When we last shared space I doubt
> I was even aware of his presence—
> a victim of his oblivion, and my own,
> well before the fact of graduation.
>
> In fifth grade, however—
> the week of Spring Camp—
> I met his eyes as the door
> of a gym locker opened,
>
> the locker in which I hid.
> His motley gang of six
> was there to find "the runt"
> and "beat him to a pulp."
>
> A counselor's timely rounds
> were my salvation that night.
>
> I look beyond Ron's graying lip
> and into his eyes once more;
> they are blue. Does he remember?
> Does it matter? After forty years
>
> I decide that it does not.
> And this afternoon

Ron Buehler himself
is the agent of my deliverance.

Life becomes art that imitates life—and dovetails with my own.

"Behold, I stand at the door and knock." Indeed.

∎

The Imitation Game

"Seriously, Greg. If you knew Putin was about to annihilate 100 or 200,000 people with a nuke, and you could stop him with a bullet to the head, wouldn't you?"

This question, or something quite like it, was posed to me during a recent social media exchange. The context doesn't take much explanation.

I have lost track of the conversation, though, and can't duplicate the query with precision, because I have taken my sweet time to compose a response. I could have dashed off one in the moment... but that's exactly part of the problem. Many of the world's greatest dilemmata are the result of unmeasured responses, of gut-reaction words or actions that tend to exacerbate already fraught tensions.

So I weighed the words and lost the moment.

I recaptured the moment last night by finally getting around to watching the Oscar-nominated 2014 film *The Imitation Game*, featuring two of our most type-cast actors, Benedict Cumberbatch (here playing, guess what, a heady and repressed homosexual who is annoyingly condescending to almost everyone around him) and Keira Knightley (here beautifully playing, guess what, a woman whose intelligence and strength make beauty irrelevant yet somehow prerequisite for the way in which she physically and/or mentally intimidates the men around her).

This explains why I took so long to see the movie. In terms of characterization and performance, I pretty much knew what to expect.

I did not expect the film to turn my mind back to the question of Putin.

So here, thanks to *The Imitation Game*, are my responses to the question.

First, I would hope that we would expect our pastors (of whom I am one) to respond, "No, of course not"—even if we have no supposed personal use for pastors. I, of course, know many fellow pastors who would reply either, "I'd have to think long and hard about that," or, "Yes," for various reasons, none of which I will take time to argue with here. I will just say that if at least some of our pastors cannot take the words of Christ at face value and seriously, and without various equivocations, we, as a species and culture, are very definitely lost and likely doomed.

Second, my favorite artistic statement on the subject comes from none other than Stephen King, who wrote *The Dead Zone* to explore the question of moral complicity. His literary conclusion: It is important to act, but it is also important to remember that evil exposed is evil emasculated, and one cannot discount the role of Providence in justice.

Third, and theologically, I can echo Clint Eastwood's Will Munny (*Unforgiven*) and observe, "It ain't about deserving." If I can be grateful for the grace which has allowed me to escape what I deserve (and I'm not talking about "sin" here, *per se*, but real and honest transgression which very much demands some kind of justice) then I have to embrace a theological system in which the sun also rises and the rain also falls on both the just and the unjust. Unless I embrace the rank-ordering of abominations, which is itself an abomination, Putin deserves as much grace as do you or I, and is no more (or less) deserving of a bullet to the head than you or I.

Fourth, and philosophically, I have to observe that Putin is not the only culprit. Even if we entirely throw out pastoral and theological considerations, we are left with this: Putin no more rises from the void than did Hitler, Mao, or Stalin. (Or others; but I'll get to that.) Getting rid of those three genocidal autocrats has not rid the world of genocide or autocracy or saved countless millions more from pointless and horrific deaths. Because what has been behind the rise of all genocidal demagoguery is our own collective lust for comfort, wealth, and power. I can refer you to historians like Heather Cox Richardson, *et al*, for very concise summaries of the ways in which Western economic and social considerations (as well as rather misguided if possibly well-meaning but certainly punitive retribution in the wake of World War I) gave rise to our notable 20th century genocides. Here, I will simply note that, following the fall of the Soviet Union, you and I and our appetites have led directly to Putin's rise and Russia's current war on Ukraine. Certainly, without Western investment in developing a global market for Russian energy resources, economic pressure might have led Putin into doing something homicidal sooner than later; but there is no question that the billions of dollars that continue to be exchanged for Russian energy products have funded and continue to fund a great deal of bloodshed.

And this is because we don't want to pay $150 to drive to Wenatchee. It's because we don't want to pay $2500 for a plane ticket to NYC. It's because we don't want to pay $5 for a plump, ripe tomato. It's because we don't want to have to choose between our Disney+ subscription and heat for the winter, or our dying daughter's prescriptions. We want our comfort, and we want it relatively cheap.

Our politicians know that, and so they kowtow to nations and leaders they know are shady (even when they are our own). They would rather stay in office by satisfying us than do the right thing at our literal expense.

So really, if anyone is to blame for Putin, it's not Putin. It's us. All of us. Not just Americans, but people everywhere. We are all alike. Without some sort of spiritual intervention—and even with it, most often—we are greedy, lazy, and morally suspect. If anyone deserves to be shot, it's all of us.

So why shoot Putin, when you should, really, shoot yourself?

Or, you could do something about yourself that would warrant a moral superiority significant enough to earn the right to hold the executioner's pistol. If you like, I can hold your beer while you make the attempt.

Finally, though, *The Imitation Game* added this socio-political response: The question is an artificial one, a straw man, because it presumes the question has never been asked or answered.

You might as well have asked, for instance: If you knew Harry Truman was about to order the extermination of 100 or 200,000 Japanese citizens and had the chance to stop him, wouldn't you put a bullet through his brain? No, of course you wouldn't. We didn't.

Or, in the case of Britain's MI-6, if you had in your possession the knowledge to stop the death of any number of innocent civilians because you had broken Hitler's Enigma message encoding, wouldn't you?

Or would you let countless people die because you were playing the longer game, not worrying about those who might die today in favor of ending the war years sooner than it might have otherwise?

The MI-6 gamble paid off, as did Truman's. In the long run, fewer people, overall, died. Perhaps not the "right" ones, from one's particular point of view, but fewer. And the moral questions turned out, as they always turn out, to be far more complex than the simple black-and-white they seemed to be.

At the socio-political level.

But I am not a politician, and I am not a philosopher. Nor am I a purely academic and cold-hearted theologian, nor a socio-political pessimist who sees voluntary human extinction as the only really plausible solution.

And while the artistic answer appeals to me, I am primarily a pastor.

Why would you ever ask me if I would shoot the most destructive of my sheep?

■

Simple Men

> Ned, there's no such thing as adventure. There's no such thing as romance. There's only trouble and desire.

Halfway through my screening of Hal Hartley's *Simple Men* the other day, those lines shot through me like... well, like a shot.

Perhaps more than other Hartley films, *Simple Men* is disarming. So much so that when the payoff comes, it almost takes your breath away.

On the surface, the film is about stasis, and about the difficulty in breaking away from the inertia that tends to hold us all in place. Bill (Robert John Burke) and his brother Dennis (Bill Sage) are trapped by the legacy of a dad on the lam, and Kate (Karen Sillas) is trapped by her history with a violent husband who has just been released from prison. Bill and Dennis are trying to find their father; Kate is trying to avoid being found by her husband. And through the happenstance which brings Kate and Bill together, the two find a strange hope for a new future.

And reconciliation with the past.

But there's so much more going on here, too. We also have, I think, Hartley himself working out how he feels about hope, fate, adventure, romance, and desire. And trouble.

Bill is not his proxy, though; that role belongs to Ned Rifle, a character named for Hartley's creative alter ego in real life. Does that make any sense? (Whatever. It's true.) And Robert John Burke, who Hartley always seems to mistake for a priest, is here, via Bill, a counselor for Hartley—one who starts out oh-so-cynical, but who also, through his hopeful encounter with Kate, has his cynicism deflowered.

So sure: He counsels Ned that "there's no such thing as adventure" and that there's "no such thing as romance. There's only trouble and desire."

> Ned: Trouble and desire?
>
> Bill: That's right, and the funny thing is when you desire something you immediately get in trouble, and when you're in trouble you don't desire anything at all.
>
> Ned: I see.
>
> Bill: It's impossible.
>
> Ned: It's ironic.
>
> Bill: It's a [effing] tragedy, is what it is, Ned.

But, as they say, the story doesn't end here. In fact, it's just getting started, and Bill really has not yet learned a thing about desire, or about real trouble—the kind of trouble that counts, the kind that makes you stay awake at night and question everything to which you have been committed.

The real tragedy is that Bill never gets to find Ned again and tell him—tell him what he's discovered about *movement*, and about grace. About desire that rocks you to your core, beauty and peace that move your soul. About letting go. About the crazy way our world always brings things full circle.

Perhaps, though, I'm wrong about all that. Perhaps there's just something ineffable here about Sillas and Burke, about the strangeness of Elina Löwensohn and Martin Donovan, about the simplicity of Sage, about the chemistry developed by all of the above and Hal Hartley while they were in college and how that works out on film, or about the way my life has intersected with this film.

I honestly cannot explain why the desire-and-trouble scene has always resonated with me. I saw *Simple Men* when it played in theaters thirty years ago and re-watched it on video a couple times after that. But when I saw that scene again after twenty-some years the other day, it was as if it had been engraved on my heart. I didn't feel like I was watching a film. I felt like I was watching tears of sorrow and joy that *I*, not Hartley, had written, and owned.

Those—and the scripted lines that bracket the film, opening and closing with the same two words.

    Don't move.

Those—and that strange non-sequitur dance sequence with Löwensohn, Donovan, Burke, and Sage, all moving Bill into Kate's arms.

I'm not exactly sure what it means to be "effable." But Art like *this* is ineffable.

■

Herb Alpert

I have not wept uncontrollably for more than four years.

The last time it happened, my heart was broken. This time it was for bittersweet joy.

Having despaired of finding anything new or interesting to watch on Netflix or Amazon Prime, I filtered through the list of documentaries available on Peacock the other evening... and stumbled across the documentary *Herb Alpert is...*

The 2020 film was directed by John Scheinfeld, who is responsible for writing and directing dozens of documentaries about musicians over the last couple of decades, some of which I had already seen.

But I didn't know that at the time, and I didn't care. I was just stunned to run across a documentary about the one-time ubiquitous Alpert, leader of the also one-time ubiquitous Tijuana Brass.

If you grew up anywhere in America in the 1960s and early 1970s, you couldn't get away from Herb Alpert and the Tijuana Brass... and most likely you didn't want to! The catchy and infectious mix of electric guitars and mariachi-style brass had everyone's attention in those days, the unusual instrumental arrangements regularly finding their way to the top of the pop charts and outselling The Beatles... while the moptops were still recording albums. If you can believe that.

For my part, I regularly listened to the five or six of the band's first eight LPs that my parents owned.

Just after my fifth birthday, *Herb Alpert's Ninth* was released. I caught sight of the LP as my mom and I walked into a Great Falls department store. The album jacket's background was a bright green and featured headshots of both Alpert and a glowering Beethoven. I already knew who Beethoven was and what his ninth symphony was; I knew Alpert and adored his music; and I got the joke.

I turned to my mom and said, "Can we get the new record?"

We could, and we did. My folks still have it, along with the other Alpert LPs.

I continued to dig the Tijuana Brass throughout my life.

My senior year in high school, my Spanish-class comrades and I shot a ten-minute short film, *Llamarada Gloria*, and I copped Alpert tunes for the film score.

While in college, I stumbled across a boxed set of the albums at a garage sale, which enabled me to have my own set and leave the original LPs to my folks.

During the years I wrote, filmed, and edited my sixty-minute Western *Who Shall Stand*, I listened constantly to an Alpert playlist. When Steve Bevens was working on the film score, I demoed Alpert tracks as models for Bevens' compositions.

Today, many of the tunes are on the summer tourist playlist in my Western-themed hat and ironwork shop The Iron Horse in Winthrop, Washington.

I have never stopped listening to Alpert, and the music has never ceased to move me.

Why?

"It's the happiest music in existence," says musician/producer Questlove. He's absolutely right.

Actor/musician Billy Bob Thornton echoed my own experience growing up with Alpert's music.

"I was raised pretty poor in the South," he says. "I always put his records on when I needed to forget everything else. Like, it could transport me into a world where I wasn't thinking about all the horrible stuff."

That was sorely needed in the Cold War years during which Martin Luther King, Jr., and Bobby Kennedy were shot, when Viet Nam was on the nightly news, when Kent State and the Democratic National Convention and Tricky Dick captured headlines. Woodstock and the Grateful Dead were balms; but so was Herb Alpert.

One interesting thing I discovered through interviews with Alpert in the film is that the effect was not really by design. That is, Alpert was not trying to write and record music that moved other people. He was not attempting to be a hit factory churning out musical ear-candy. "It has to feel good," says Alpert of his art. "I think that's the ingredient. ... If something touches you, it touches you on a very deep level. I don't think people listen with their ears. I think they listen with their soul."

So part of the effect came from Alpert's philosophy of music. Another came from what he learned from other musicians with whom he had worked, such as Sam Cooke: "It ain't what you do. It's the way and how you do it."

By the time he cut his first album with the newly formed Tijuana Brass, a concept based on these principles was already fully formed in his twenty-four-year-old brain. And around that concept he wrapped an instrumental sound inspired by The Beatles' overdubbed vocals and the vibe of a Tijuana bull ring.

The effect was musical magic and a financial bonanza.

"I never tried to make a hit record," he confirms. "I always tried to make a good record, a fun record. Something that's interesting to listen to. For me, not for anyone else."

It just so happened that America also loved what moved Alpert.

And so lots of Americans, and scads of kids like Billy Bob Thornton and I, developed a lot of misconceptions about the band and the music. For instance, the Alpert sound is not representative at all of Mexican (or even Tijuanan) music. It's a jazzy hybrid of Alpert's own invention that has never really been duplicated. As musician after musician can confirm for you, when you hear Alpert's music you always know it's Alpert. It can never be confused with someone else's.

For another thing… Alpert isn't Mexican. Not even Mexican-American. Nor remotely Hispanic. His father was a pre-war Jewish immigrant from the Ukraine, of all things.

We can be forgiven for the confusion, says Thornton. "They always wore the Mexican little short jackets and stuff. It's called the Tijuana Brass," he smirkingly relates, again mirroring my own experience. "Why the hell would we *not* think he's Mexican?"

> So I grew up thinking his real name was probably something like Alberto Martinez and he just changed it to Herb Alpert, you know, and so I thought, "This is so cool—this Mexican cat, he lives in L.A. and, you know, but he brought his music here."

So that's the source of the joyous part of my sobbing.

The bittersweet part comes from learning about the rest of the story—how the sudden and overwhelming success broke Alpert's own heart and spirit, how for years he couldn't even play a note, how he had to not only learn how to play again, but how to love and live again... without the spotlight, without the "success," without the family of brilliant artists that he and Jerry Moss gathered to A&M records.

"All of a sudden I was catapulted into this thing from one hit record into many hit records," he says. "At that point I realized, 'Man, I have the American dream come true. I'm famous, I'm rich, but I'm miserable.'"

But what he gained instead in the wake of all that... Oh, what he gained. You'll have to see the film yourself for that beautiful tale. No spoilers from me.

My wife Misuk was watching some of this film in the background while she was preparing a meal. She grew up in Korea and didn't come to the United States until long after Alpert's music had migrated from mainstream to Muzak.

As the final credits started to crawl, intrigued by what she had seen, she asked, "Who is that man?"

Herb Alpert is…

And I just started to bawl. Until that moment I did not understand the depths to which Alpert's music had touched my soul and for how long. The tears would not stop, and I did not want them to.

It was the first time Misuk has seen me cry like that, and the beauty was that she understood where the tears came from. She had seen enough of the film, and she knew of my affinity for his music.

Alpert is still alive. Yes, indeed. His foundation still does wonderful, wonderful things for people around the world, and he still sculpts, paints, and makes music.

I am so glad this wonderful world contains artists like Alpert.

■

Miss American Pie

"I was as surprised as anyone that I could make magic," says Don McLean.

If you grew up in the 1970s and at all listened to the radio—and who didn't, when the only entertainment options were books, three networks and one local TV station (plus PBS), and your transistor or car radio?—you couldn't escape McLean's iconic tune "American Pie," whether you liked it or not. And to be honest, not everybody liked it.

But everybody liked talking about it. After all, what's it mean? There's a story in there, but it's a psychobabble mishmash that begins with a paperboy reading the headlines about Buddy Holly, Ritchie Valens, and the Big Bopper, and then takes eight minutes before it winds up with the Holy Trinity on a heartland train headed to Hollywood. Verses are interspersed with a nonsense chorus—drunkards singing about death alongside a riverbed... which was quite dry, even if the good ol' boys weren't.

How is it that such a counterintuitive and anti-pop tune dominated the airwaves and music charts for an entire summer and remains a cultural touchstone fifty years later?

Mark Moorman's documentary *The Day the Music Died* actually provides a very satisfactory answer—or a set of answers—to that question. Bolstered by reputable and relevant opinion-havers like Garth Brooks and Peter Gallagher, Don McLean and track producer Ed Freeman yield a ton of first-hand insight into the making of the song. To a certain extent, it was simply a question of timing, *a propos* for a piece of music: the right musician connecting with the right people and the right producer at the right time, with the right studio musicians, to make a singular bit of studio magic that happened to hit the music business at the right time to connect with a generation of iconoclasts who really didn't give a rip what pop songs were "supposed" to sound like. (Remember that in the 1970s, top-40 hits were all over the map, from "Wild Thing" to Gary Glitter's "Rock and Roll" to "Spirit in the Sky" to "Nights in White Satin" to Nilsson's "Coconut" to Michael Jackson's "Ben," a horror-movie love song to a pet rat.)

Part of the fun of the documentary is debunking a lot of the speculative hoo-ha about McLean's cryptic lyrics. If you suspected that they were more straightforward than most people insisted, you'd be right. "If I were talking about Elvis, I would have mentioned Elvis," says McLean, clarifying that the middle verses are not allegorical, but are rather a metaphoric fable. And the trio that hops on the coast-bound train? For McLean, the song's actual, um, writer, it comprises the literal Father, Son, and Holy Ghost, upon whom he was raised and in whom he still retains a certain measure of faith. And, you know, they're mentioned in the actual lyrics. Mic drop.

But the film is also quite moving when it comes to explaining the cultural zeitgeist of which the song was a part. About half an hour before the end of the film, Misuk interrupted the viewing to ask me what the fuss was all about. She didn't come to the United States from Korea until the mid-1980s, so the historical setting of the writing of the song was pretty much a mystery to her.

Curiously, just after I finished explaining my take on it, we went back to the film and producer Ed Freeman explained his perspective... and he said it better than I did.

> The more I listened to it, the more I thought, wow, this is like an epic. "American Pie" was really encapsulating the experience of a whole generation. We were witness to the death of the American Dream. We went through both Kennedys being shot, Malcom X, Martin Luther King, Viet Nam.
>
> You know, hippies thought we were going to take over the world with love and peace, and it didn't happen. For me, "American Pie" is the eulogy for a dream that didn't take place.
>
> It was really important that way. I think we all needed it. It was an acknowledgement of what we had been through, and in a way—because it was an acknowledgement—we could move on.

Now, I was a couple of years behind the hippie generation; but I was certainly close enough to it to understand it, and even today, living in Washington State's Methow Valley, I'm surrounded by a host of aging hippie idealists who landed here fifty years ago and gradually watched themselves betray their dreams in small but significant steps. Or, if you like, whittled them into other shapes with which they eventually made peace.

So, yeah. Whether we liked it or not—and I did not, particularly—we all certainly engaged with the song. It affected how we saw the past and what we hoped for our futures. It was inescapable.

And so are dreams, fulfilled or otherwise.

The Day the Music Died is at the very least an extraordinarily satisfying look at Don McLean's!

∎

Whiplash

Where was I in early 2015?

Clearly not in theaters seeing the music-school gut-punch *Whiplash*. Nor was I tuning in to the Oscars telecast to see the film win a handful of well-deserved awards.

I was, however, still a film critic, so I am kind of embarrassed to only now discover this film, quite late to the party.

I started seeing it pop up in Amazon Prime recommendations a few weeks ago but managed to keep skipping over it because I am not particularly a fan of J.K. Simmons. He has always struck me as over-the-top and artificial in his performances, even when he's trying to be easygoing (as in those insurance commercials). After watching the trailer, however, I decided to check it out.

Now, I have written in the past about my love affair with jazz and swing. After living the dream through my sophomore year of high school, I quit the program because of the petty, childish, and abusive behavior of the band director, Greg Goss. A prerequisite to perform in the (extracurricular) jazz band was participation in the regular concert band—and it was there that Goss emotionally blackmailed students to cater to his musical whims via calculated and histrionic temper tantrums. I and several other students quit in protest.

Not that the protest did any good.

The Foster High School jazz band was pretty sweet, though, and curiously, Goss performed no antics with this group. We were an award-winning combo right out of the gate and played together like a well-oiled trombone slide. We all put in the long extra hours outside of school necessary to reap the sweet rewards of performance.

And still... the poison of concert band made a screening of *Whiplash* feel like a PTSD nightmare.

In the film, ass-hat band leader Terence Fletcher (Simmons) recruits drummer Andrew Neiman out of a flagship music academy's plebian ranks to join the school's elite "studio band." The entire idea is to find a drummer who can deliver Fletcher's double-time dream performance of the classic Wasson arrangement of Duke Ellington's "Caravan." The problem that quickly develops is that Fletcher is not only emotionally and physically abusive with the students, he is also such a mind-rapist that neither Neiman nor the viewers are ever sure exactly what Fletcher is after. It's only Neiman's absolute love for the music that keeps him in this game.

And this is where I departed from this scenario in real life. Music was about the only thing keeping me going when I was fourteen; and leaving it remains one of the hardest things I have done in my life. But... I was not willing, as is Andrew Neiman in *Whiplash*, to push myself nearly to the point of death just so some egomaniac could use me as a stepladder to a higher-profile and better-paying job.

Fletcher's ass-hat at least has the excuse that he's trying to create another Charlie Parker using the same ass-hat methods that (supposedly) turned a fumbling Parker into the legendary

"Bird." Greg Goss, as far as I am aware, never had such an excuse. He simply fell into the self-indulgent stereotype of abusive ass-hat artists because, well, you know, brilliant artists must be indulged (or at least tolerated, because, gosh, you know, where would we be without them?).

Right.

But what sets *Whiplash* apart from other excellent films is its closing act, which musically justifies the preceding carnage—and poses a pair of really fairly difficult questions, for neither of which do I have particularly good answers. To wit:

First: If a musician (or performance) of true genius is spawned by the upstream struggle of swimming in a Fletcher-esque river, is the river perhaps justified? Does it even need justification, or is it simply a necessary force of nature which salmon are doomed to seek?

Second: Who's really pushing whom in such a scenario? Is it possible that the salmon is actually shaping the river, too, while the river arrogantly thinks it holds all the cards?

Now, I was not at all surprised to learn that *Whiplash*, Damien Chazelle's warm-up effort for Best Picture winner *La La Land*, was inspired by Chazelle's own experiences in high school jazz band. The damn thing just feels too lived-in to be anything else, as stylized as it may be.

So... if you have a hankering to help work through your own musical trauma, *Whiplash* might be of help.

Or, if you want some insight into the maniacal pursuits of obsessed musi-cians, *Whiplash* is a good start.

Outside of those two objectives... wow, I don't know. The primary reaction you are likely to have is, "What the bloody hell!" I am not surprised to learn that the film only grossed $13 million in its theatrical release here in the States. It's far too intense a film to be broadly popular.

I am also not surprised that the film's second-highest gross came in South Korea, at $11 million. As I have learned via my Korean wife, it's not just musical excellence that is pursued by young people there with this kind of life-or-death intensity. Music... art... math... everything. *Whiplash* is simply a metaphor for the trainwreck of life as a Korean youth.

Wowza.

■

Never Cry Wolf

Chip on the shoulder much?

In 2011, I was flown to Clearwater, Florida, to cover the release of *Dolphin Tale*, the heartwarming film about Winter, the dolphin who, in real life, had her tail damaged and learned to use a prosthetic.

The film was directed by Charles Martin Smith—a tremendous artist who has mostly flown under the radar for the bulk of his career... though most everyone has seen *American Graffiti* (in which he played one of the leads, Terry the Toad) and *The Untouchables* (in which he held his own with costars Robert DeNiro, Sean Connery, Kevin Costner, and Andy Garcia... all of them decked out in Armani).

During his career he has worked with some of the greatest film artists: De Palma, Coppola, Lucas, and so on.

But there is one film he carried pretty much on his own (excepting a brief supporting turn by Brian Dennehy, and some canines)—Carroll Ballard's *Never Cry Wolf*, based on the writings of Farley Mowat. The film tells the story of a wet-behind-the-ears Canadian biologist who takes a suicidal assignment from his government to study wolves in their natural habitat. In the most remote regions of the Arctic. In the winter.

The cynical point of the study—turned to graceful and moving beauty by the protagonist, and by Mowat and Ballard—is to fund work that cannot possibly be completed, so that the prevailing wisdom about the decline of caribou populations may continue to prevail and the further slaughter of wolves be justified.

The tagline of the film:

> They thought he couldn't do the job. That's why they chose him.

I saw the film in Seattle during its limited theatrical run in 1984 and was apparently one of twenty or so other people who did. I of course loved it; it is perhaps the single film that most nearly captures the spirit of my own love affair with nature (and sarcastic wit).

But I don't remember seeing the version of the movie poster, at the time, that included that tag line. I didn't see that until much later, probably 1992, when I was in Orlando on a business trip introducing the new product I had just completed managing for Quinton Instrument Company. While visiting Universal Studios, I stopped in to the movie memorabilia shop just inside the gates and ran across the original press kit for *Never Cry Wolf:* a 40-page glossy oversized magazine including interviews with Ballard, Mowat, Smith, and others. The cover was a reproduction of the tag-lined movie poster.

"They thought he couldn't do the job. That's why they chose him."

Such irony. I had just spent four grueling years of work on a job at which everyone outside the engineering department had expected me—a twenty-something rookie project manager tackling the most important project in the company's history—to fail. Nobody else wanted to touch the project and be potentially responsible for its failure. Like Tyler in the film, I didn't know any better—or how badly I was being set up to fail.

So I naturally snapped up that (very collectible) press kit, had it framed, and for the rest of my engineering career had it proudly displayed on the wall in my office.

Yeah. Major chip on the shoulder.

So when I found out I would have one-on-one time with Mr. Smith in Clearwater, I did a most unprofessional thing, a major no-no in the press industry. I brought along a piece of memorabilia for Smith to sign. For one lone day in my winding-down second career as a film critic, I was going to be a fanboy. Sheesh.

The extended time I got to spend with Smith was delightful, however, and for both of us. The interview covered far more than *Dolphin Tale*, his career, or *Never Cry Wolf*. We discussed the philosophy of art, the strengths of various film directors, family, and our personal preferences in literature and film.

By the end of our time together, I did not feel at all bashful about trotting out the press kit for *Never Cry Wolf* and handing Smith a Sharpie.

In some ways, my talk with Smith brought some closure to the resentment I felt for nearly twenty years.

But just today I finished setting up my new office at Caisteal Westfernesse, and the last things I hung on the walls were my diplomas... and that signed and framed press kit. They have been in storage for a very long time.

And I have to tell you... I still got a little surge of pride and a little tug of resentment. I long ago learned not to take overmuch credit for "my" achievements... but boy, for a time did I relish the identity of The Guy Who Could Defy the Odds.

Yeah. Wonderstruck.

∎

Acknowledgements

There is no timeline for grief, but for me the two years following Jenn's tragic and magical passing were the crucible. I am indebted to those who were closest to me throughout my renaissance of joy:
- My oldest friend, Stephanie Cortes, always a trusted companion, who helped talk me through Jenn's hospice decline and beyond;
- My sister, Elane Rosok, who has always understood me, even when she tormented me as a child;
- Peter Alford, whose own life was in great flux as he encountered the closing months of mine and Jenn's, and who talked long and weekly with me for many years following Jenn's death;
- Fellow high school alumnus Denise Driscoll, who re-entered my life at just the right time to help get both my physical and spiritual bodies back in shape;
- College roommate John Adami, who has always seemed to have his forefinger on my spiritual pulse and re-enter my life at just the right times;

- Kaileah Akker, whose youthful energy and spiritual sensitivity have been invaluable in my journey on the eastern slope of the Cascades;
- Subhaga Crystal Bacon, whose friendship has encouraged a six-year outpouring of poetry and prose, and who provided the final nudge to collect these essays;
- and most of all, my wife, Misuk Ko, whose keen questions and close reading of my essays have taught me that I do not need to say (or write) everything that passes through my mind… just the stuff that really matters.